ᵗʰᵉREP
Birmingham Repertory Theatre

Birmingham Repertory Theatre Company
presents

the world premiere of

Only The Lonely

by Tamsin Oglesby

GW00722355

First performed on 11 November 2005
at Birmingham Repertory Theatre

Birmingham Repertory Theatre
Centenary Square
Broad Street
Birmingham
B1 2EP

www.birmingham-rep.co.uk.

Birmingham Repertory Theatre Company presents

Only The Lonely

by Tamsin Oglesby

Cast in order of speaking

Joe Mikey Lightfoot

Bill Jonathan Coyne

Michelle
Sarah-Jane Drummey

Henry Benjamin Whitrow

Liza Ann Firbank

Clint Peter Eastland

Director Lynne Parker

Set and Lighting Design
John Comiskey

Sound Designer Fergus O'Hare

Stage Manager Jane Bullock

Deputy Stage Manager
Nina Scholar

With thanks to

Immingham Railfreight Terminals Ltd,
Stallingborough

autism . west midlands

The Cast

Bill
Jonathan Coyne

Theatre credits include: *Richard II* (Ludlow Castle); *Battle Of Green Lanes* (Theatre Royal Stratford East); *Messiah* (Old Vic); *Macbeth* (BAC); *Communicating Doors* (Worcester Swan): *The Old Curiosity Shop* (Southwark Playhouse); *Cinderella* (Lyric Hammersmith); *A Country Wife* (Wolsey Ipswich); *A Midsummer Night's Dream* (English Shakespeare Company/tour); *Twelfth Night* and *Love Is A Drug* (Oxford Stage Company); *Lysistrata* (Contact Manchester); *Smoke* (Royal Exchange); *The New Apartment* (BAC); *A Slight Case Of Murder* (Nottingham Playhouse); *One Flew Over The Cuckoo's Nest* (New Vic); *The Little Heroine* (Nuffield Southampton); *The Glass Menagerie* (Century Theatre); *Arturo Ui* (Liverpool Everyman); *Faust* parts 1&2 (Citizens Glasgow); *Rosencrantz And Guildernstern Are Dead* (Latchmere Theatre); *The Importance Of Being Earnest* (Edinburgh Lyceum) and *Bent* (Theatr Clwyd).

Television credits include: *Casualty*, *EastEnders*, *Seriously Funny*, *The Bill*, *Gulliver's Travels*, *Preston Front* and *London's Burning*.

Film includes: *Tomb Raider*, *I'll Sleep When I'm Dead* and *Secrets And Lies*.

Radio includes: *The Rover*.

Michelle
Sarah-Jane Drummey

Theatre credits include: *The Synge Cycle* (the plays of J.M. Synge) and *The Spirit Of Annie Ross* (Druid Theatre); *The Mandate* and *The Night Season* (National Theatre); *The Sanctuary Lamp* and *Big Maggie* (Abbey and Peacock Theatres); *The Drunkard* (B*spoke Theatre Company); *Emma*, *Hard Times* and *The Starchild* (Storytellers Theatre Company); *A Miracle In Ballymore* (Red Kettle Theatre Company); *This Property Is Condemned* (Bewleys Theatre); *Fado Fado* (Siamsa Tire); *Blood Wedding* (Common Currency) and *April Bright* (Fada Theatre).

Film and television includes: *Inside I'm Dancing*, *Bloom*, *Dead Bodies* and *Any Time Now*.

Clint
Peter Eastland

Peter was born in Exeter and trained at the Webber Douglas Academy.

Theatre credits include: *Mourning Becomes Electra, Three Sisters, The Cherry Orchard, The Winter's Tale* and *The Relapse* (National Theatre); *The Wedding* (Young Vic); *Waterfall* and *Rosencrantz And Guildenstern Are Dead* (for Vanessa Redgrave's Moving Theatre Company at The Riverside Studios Hammersmith, The Dramski Theatre Skopje and on a tour of Former Yugoslavia); *Northanger Abbey* (Theatre Royal, Northampton); *Over A Barrel, Metamorphosis, Romeo And Juliet, A Midsummer Night's Dream* and *Dangerous Liaisons* (Everyman, Cheltenham); *The Love Child* (Red Shift) and *Far From The Madding Crowd* (King's Head, London).

Television includes: *Waking The Dead, Casualty, Small Potatoes* and co-presenting CBBC's summer activity series *Telequest*.

Film includes *Inside The Wolf's Lair* with Sean Bean.

Joe
Mikey Lightfoot

Mikey Lightfoot is 13 years old and was born in Redditch, Worcestershire. He is a member of Birmingham Repertory Theatre's Young REP youth theatre company.

Theatre credits include: Chip in *Beauty And The Beast* (Birmingham Hippodrome); Tiny Tim in *A Christmas Carol* (Birmingham Alexandra Theatre); *The Wizard Of Oz, Ridin' The No 8* and *Brassed Off* (Birmingham Repertory Theatre) as well as various productions at Birmingham's Crescent Theatre. Mikey has also danced at 'Young World' concerts in Newcastle, Manchester, Birmingham and Sheffield.

Television includes: *Doctors*.

Mikey will be working with the National Youth Theatre in 2006

The Cast

Liza
Ann Firbank

Theatre credits include: *Macbeth* (Almeida); *Becket* (Haymarket); *Three Women* (Riverside); *Maps Of Desire* (Wonderful Beast at Southwark Playhouse); *Dance Of Death* (Lyric); *Habitat* and *The Candidate* (Manchester Royal Exchange); *Les Liasons Dangereuses* (Liverpool Playhouse); *Henry V* and *Comedy Of Errors* (RSC); *Much Ado About Nothing* (Cheek By Jowl, Playhouse, European tour & BAM New York); *Hedda Gabler* (English Touring Theatre/Donmar); *Macbeth, A Working Woman, Tess Of The D'Urbervilles, Postcards From Rome* (West Yorkshire Playhouse); *The Winter's Tale* and *Romeo & Juliet* (AFTLS/USA Touring); *Mary Stuart* by Dacia Maraini (BAC); *A Handful Of Dust* (Shared Experience/Lyric Hammersmith); *Celestina, Ion, Orpheus, The Belle Vue* (ATC/Lyric Studio); *God Say Amen* (English Shakespeare Co.); *The Old Devils* (Theatre Clwyd/tour); *High Society* (Victoria Palace); *Julius Caesar* and *The York Mysteries* (National Theatre); *The Invisible Woman* and *A Little Satire* (Gate); *Twelfth Night, Richard III, Antony And Cleopatra* (Stratford Festival, Ontario); *The Hollow Crown* (RSC Aldwych/World Tour); *Their Very Own* and *Golden City, The Voysey Inheritance, The Pleasure Principle* (Royal Court).

Television credits include: *Elizabeth, Doctors, Heartbeat, Poirot, Kavanagh QC, Boon, Heart Of The Country, Growing Rich, Mother Love, Flesh And Blood, Lillie, The Nearly Man, Persuasion, Hotel du Lac, 10th Kingdom, An Evil Streak, Surgical Spirits, Animal Ark, The Goodguys, Crown Court, Emergency Ward 10, Kenilworth.*

Film credits include: *Anna And The King, A Passage To India, Esther Kahn, Strapless, Lionheart, The Magic Box, A Severed Head, Asylum, Accident, Sunday Bloody Sunday, Darling, The Servant, Carry On Nurse.*

Henry
Benjamin Whitrow

This is Benjamin's first return to Birmingham since 1965 when he was at the Old Rep under John Harrison. After that he joined the National Theatre Company at The Old Vic, where he appeared in: *Rosencrantz And Guildenstern Are Dead, Amphitron, Volpone, H, The Idiot, Home And Beauty, A Flea In Her Ear, The Merchant Of Venice, School For Scandal, The Front Page, Twelfth Night* and *Next Of Kin*. Other theatre credits include *Otherwise Engaged* (Queen's Theatre); *Dirty Linen* (Arts Theatre); *The Wild Duck* (Guildford); *Ten Times Table* (Globe); *The Last Of Mrs Cheyney* and *Terra Nova* (Chichester); *Passion Play* (Aldwych); *The Portage To Sanchristobel* (Mermaid); *The Cherry Orchard* (Haymarket); *Noises Off* (Savoy); *A Little Hotel On The Side* (National Theatre); *Made In Bankok* (Aldwych); *A Man For All Seasons* (Chichester); *Uncle Vanya* (Vaudeville); *A Little Love* (Lyric Hammersmith); *The Sisterhood, Henry VIII* and *Preserving Mr Panmuir* (Chichester); *Racing Demon* (National Theatre); *The Winters Tale* and *The Merry Wives Of Windsor* (RSC); *Forty Years On* (West Yorkshire Playhouse); *Loot* (Palace Theatre Watford); *Wild Oats, The Invention Of Love* (RNT); *Equally Divided* (Duncan Wheldon Prods); *The Young Idea* (Chester Gateway); *The Rivals* and *Henry IV Part 2* (RSC); *What The Butler Saw* (Old Vic) and *The Lady's Not For Burning* (Chichester).

Television includes: *Poirot: After The Funeral, Margaret, Murder In Suburbia, We Think The World Of You, Hayfever, Minor Complications, On Approval, The Factory, Troilus And Cressida, Bergerac, A Moment In Time, A Crack In The Ice, Shackleton, Paying Guests, Victoria Wood, One Fine Day, Partners In Crime, Coming Through, Starlite Ballroom, Spoils Of War, All For Love, Ffizz, Pastoral Care, Natural Causes, Harry's Game, Tales Of The Unexpected, Chancer, The New Statesman, A Few Selected Exits, Peak Practice, Moving Story, Men Of The World, Pride And Prejudice, The Bill, The Merchant Of Venice, Inspector Morse, Embassy, Tom Jones, Blonde Bombshell, Kiss Me Kate, Jonathan Creek, Other People's Children, Midsomer Murders, Monarch Of The Glenn* and *Henry VIII.*

Film includes: *Sauce For The Goose, Sharma And Beyond, A Man For All Seasons, Brimstone And Treacle, Clockwise, A Shocking Accident, On The Black Hill, Personal Services, Charlie, Damage, Project Samurai, Restoration, The Saint, Golden Afternoon, The Opium Wars, Jilting Joe, Chicken Run* and *Scenes Of A Sexual Nature*

The Creative Team

Tamsin Oglesby
Author

Tamsin is currently under commission to the National Theatre and Hampstead Theatre.

Her other plays include: *U.S. And Them* (first performed at Hampstead Theatre); *Olive* (a play for children, commissioned and presented under the National Theatre's Shell Connections initiative); *Two Lips Indifferent Red* (first performed at the Bush Theatre) and *My Best Friend* (commissioned by Birmingham Repertory Theatre and performed at The REP and Hampstead Theatre.

Previously, Tamsin worked as a director, and directed and devised plays at the Royal Court, National Studio and extensively on the London Fringe, receiving nominations for the Young Director Award 1990 and for Best Production *Grave Plots* at the London Fringe Awards 1990.

Tamsin has written a number of radio plays and is currently developing one-off and series ideas for television.

Lynne Parker
Director

Lynne is co-founder and Artistic Director of Rough Magic Theatre Company. Productions for Rough Magic include *Top Girls*, *Decadence*, *The Country Wife*, *Nightshade*, *Spokesong*, *Serious Money*, *Aunt Dan And Lemon*, *The Tempest*, *Tom And Viv*, *Lady Windermere's Fan*, *Digging For Fire*, *Love And A Bottle*, *I Can't Get Started*, *New Morning*,

Danti-Dan, *Down Onto Blue*, *The Dogs*, *Hidden Charges*, *Halloween Night*, *The Way Of The World*, *Pentecost*, *Northern Star*, *The School For Scandal*, *The Whisperers*, *Boom-town*, *Three Days Of Rain*, *Dead Funny*, *Midden*, *Copenhagen* (Best Production, Irish Times/ESB Irish Theatre Awards), *Shiver*, *Olga*, *Take Me Away*, *Improbable Frequency* (Best Production and Best Director, Irish Times/ESB Irish Theatre Awards) and *The Life Of Galileo*.

Productions at the Abbey and Peacock Theatres include *The Trojan Women*, *The Doctor's Dilemma*, *Tartuffe*, *Down The Line*, *The Sanctuary Lamp*, *The Drawer Boy* (Galway Arts Festival co-production), *The Shape Of Metal* and *Heavenly Bodies* (Best Director, Irish Times/ESB Irish Theatre Awards).

Other work outside the company includes productions for Druid, Tinderbox, Opera Theatre Company and 7:84 Scotland, and Lynne was an Associate Artist of Charabanc for whom she adapted and directed *The House Of Bernarda Alba*. Lynne has also directed *The Clearing* (Bush Theatre); *The Playboy Of The Western World*, *The Silver Tassie* and *Our Father* (Almeida Theatre); *Brothers Of The Brush* (Arts Theatre); *The Shadow Of A Gunman* (Gate, Dublin); *Playhouse Creatures* (The Peter Hall Company at the Old Vic); *The Importance Of Being Earnest* (West Yorkshire Playhouse); *Love Me?!* (Corn Exchange's Car Show); *The Comedy Of Errors* (RSC); *Olga And Shimmer* (Traverse Theatre, Edinburgh) and *The Drunkard* (b*spoke Theatre Company).

John Comiskey
Set and Lighting Design

John's recent theatre work includes set and lighting designs for *Hamlet* (Peacock & Lyric Theatres); *Mermaids* (CoisCéim Dance Theatre) and *Copenhagen* for which he won an Irish Theatre Award for Best Set Design. He has designed lighting for numerous Irish theatre companies including The Abbey, Druid, Siamsa Tire, Barabbas...the company, Galloglass, Operating Theate (of which he was also an Artistic Director) and two performance works by James Coleman.

Work as a director includes *The Well* (Abhann Productions) and Gavin Friday's *Ich Liebe Dich*, both for recent Dublin Theatre Festivals, and two years as Production Director worldwide of *Riverdance – the Show* (Abhann Productions).

Film work includes directing the dance film *Hit And Run* which won the main awards at both Dance On Camera New York and Moving Pictures Toronto; documentaries on *The Dingle Wren's Day* and *The Berlin Years Of Agnes Bernelle* and the concert films *Celtic Woman*, *Brian Kennedy Live In Belfast* and *Ronan Tynan: The Impossible Dream* for PBS. He was a television director with RTÉ for twelve years, where his numerous credits included *The Eurovision Song Contest 1995*, various telethons and the inauguration of President Mary Robinson.

Fergus O'Hare
Sound

Theatre sound designs include: *Cleansed* (Oxford Stage Company); *'Tis Pity She's A Whore* (Southwark Playhouse); *Translations* (National Theatre); *Prayer Room* (Edinburgh International Festival); *Richard II*, *Philadelphia Story*, *Aladdin*, *Cloaca*, *Hamlet*, *The Tempest* and *24 Hour Plays* (Old Vic); *Shoreditch Madonna* (Soho Theatre); *This Is How It Goes* (Donmar); *On The Ceiling* (West End); *Someone Who'll Watch Over Me* (Ambassadors); *The Cosmonaut's Last Message To The Woman He Once Loved In The Former Soviet Union* (Donmar); *Hecuba* (RSC); *Dracula* (tour); *One Under* (Tricycle Theatre); *Anna In The Tropics* (Hampstead Theatre); *Vermilion Dream* (Salisbury); *Clouds* (tour); *Twelfth Night* (Albery); *Shimmer* (Traverse) *Henry IV* (Donmar); *The Quare Fellow*, *Rookery Nook*, *Easter*, *Home*, *Candida*, *Singer* and *Seargeant Musgrave's Dance* (OSC).

Work in New York, Los Angeles and Sydney includes: *The Shape Of Things*, *A Day In The Death Of Joe Egg*, *Dance Of Death*, *Noises Off* and *Electra* (Drama Desk Nominee) and *An Enemy Of The People*.

$\frac{\text{THE}}{}$REP

Birmingham Repertory Theatre

Birmingham Repertory Theatre is one of Britain's leading national theatre companies. From its base in Birmingham, The REP produces over twenty new productions each year.

The commissioning and production of new work lies at the core of The REP's programme. In 1998 the company launched The Door, a venue dedicated to the production and presentation of new work. This, together with an investment in commissioning new drama from some of Britain's brightest and best writing talent, gives The REP a unique position in British theatre. Indeed, through the extensive commissioning of new work The REP is providing vital opportunities for the young and emerging writing talent that will lead the way in the theatre of the future. The current Autumn to Spring season includes a new production of Brecht's *The Life Of Galileo* translated by David Edgar and featuring Timothy West in the lead role, *Promises And Lies* a new musical featuring the music of UB40, a new adaptation of *Three Sisters* by Mustapha Matura alongside new plays in The Door.

REP productions regularly transfer to London and also tour nationally and internationally. Over the last few years several of our productions have been seen in London including *Of Mice And Men, The Birthday Party, The Old Masters* and *The Snowman*.

Artistic Director **Jonathan Church**
Executive Director **Stuart Rogers**
Associate Director (Literary) **Ben Payne**

Box Office 0121 236 4455
Book online at www.birmingham-rep.co.uk

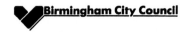 

EUROPEAN COMMUNITY

European Regional
Development Fund

The Door

The Door was established six years ago as a theatre dedicated to the production and presentation of new writing. In this time, it has given world premieres to new plays from a new generation of British playwrights including Abi Morgan, Moira Buffini, Bryony Lavery, Crispin Whittell, Paul Lucas, Gurpreet Kaur Bhatti, Sarah Woods, Amber Lone, Roy Williams, Kaite O'Reilly, Ray Grewal, Jess Walters, Nick Stafford, Jonathan Harvey, Tamsin Oglesby and Sarah Daniels. Last year, the company received The Peggy Ramsay Award for New Writing, to support the company's work in developing and commissioning new plays for the future. The programme of The Door aims to provide a distinct alternative to the work seen in the Main House: a space where new voices and contemporary stories can be heard, and that seeks to create new audiences for the work of the company in this city and beyond.

In addition to work by British writers, The Door has begun to develop collaborations with international companies and exchange new plays with theatres overseas. Another long-term aim is to broaden the diversity of the work that we present and co-produce through developing relationships with a range of companies touring and producing new writing such as Creative Origins, Out of Joint, Kali, Graeae, Paines Plough and Yellow Earth theatre companies.

The Door is also a place to explore new ideas and different approaches to making theatre, to develop new plays and support emerging companies - for example, through the theatre's *Beyond The Boundaries* project. It also emphasises work for and by young people, through *Transmissions* - our young playwright's project, our *First Stages* children's theatre programme and the strong emphasis on new work and work with living writers in *Young REP*, our youth theatre initiative.

For more information about the work of The Door or about our work with new writers, please contact Ben Payne or Caroline Jester at The REP on 0121 245 2000.

Transcriptions

Transmissions is The REP's unique project aimed at nurturing the playwrights of the future. It gives twenty young writers from across the West Midlands the chance to develop their writing skills in a constructive and creative way.

Transmissions writers are given the opportunity of working with professional playwrights to develop initial ideas into complete scripts.

The scheme allows participants to meet other writers in a fun and interactive environment, giving them the support and encouragement needed to expand their interest, but with a very definite aim; to see their work performed on stage by professional actors to a live audience.

In July the writers come together with professional actors and directors to present a showcase of their work in the Transmissions Festival.

Transmissions Outreach Programme is supported by the Paul Hamlyn Foundation, with schools from across the region participating. Professional playwrights lead workshops in schools, and extracts from plays developed by students are also performed in the summer festival in The Door.

"Transmissions hurtled into its second week, blazing with energy and delivering some of the most provocative and original new work to be seen anywhere in the city" Birmingham Post

"A rich and extraordinary assortment of tomorrow's talent" Evening Mail

"It is a brilliant enterprise" Birmingham Post

If you would like to become involved with Transmissions or want further information, please contact the **Literary Department** at The REP on **0121 245 2045**.

Tamsin Oglesby
Only the Lonely

faber and faber

First published in 2005
by Faber and Faber Limited
3 Queen Square London WC1N 3AU

Typeset by Country Setting, Kingsdown, Kent CT14 8ES
Printed in England by Mackays of Chatham plc, Chatham, Kent

A CIP record for this book
is available from the British Library

ISBN 0–571–23204–3

2 4 6 8 10 9 7 5 3 1

Characters

Joe
Michelle
Bill
Henry
Liza
Clint
Policeman
TV Voice

There are five areas of action
Bill's garden
Joe and Michelle's back yard
Joe and Michelle's front room
A train carriage
A street corner

ONLY THE LONELY

ONE

Bill is in his garden, digging. He is talking to himself.

Joe, in his backyard, exercising. Neither has noticed the other.

Joe is warming up for a karate sequence and it's only when he swivels that he sees Bill. He stops and stares. Bill becomes aware of being watched. He is unnerved and stops mumbling. His digging takes on a frantic quality.

Joe resumes his karate. At first he is focused, quiet. He repeats the same move several times.

Confident that Joe is no longer watching him now, Bill stops digging and observes Joe.

Joe begins a complicated, vigorous sequence. He attempts it several times before he's happy with it. He takes his shirt off. Bill looks away hastily, grabs at his secateurs and snips at some old foliage.

Distracted by the sound, Joe hesitates. But since Bill ignores him, he resumes his routine.

After a while, Bill stands and stretches. He sees Joe over the fence again and watches. Mesmerised by the gestures, he involuntarily mimics them with his head. Joe pretends he hasn't noticed Bill watching him. He starts showing off, aping sound effects to his moves. He is Bruce Lee now.

Bill is transfixed. Joe is graceful and strong and compelling to watch. He finishes a sequence and lands squarely opposite Bill, facing him over the fence. As if facing his audience. Bill is startled by the confrontation. He drops his trowel. Bends to pick it up. Drops it again. Picks it up again.

Joe Alright?

Bill stares at Joe. Eventually he finds the answer.

Bill Yes! (*He nods vigorously.*)

Joe Alright.

Silence. Joe throws his shirt over his shoulder and goes inside.

Once Bill's established that he's alone, he flexes his arms in imitation of one of Joe's karate routines. It is more like dance than karate; his movements are oddly graceful. He repeats the sequence until he is pleased with it.

TWO

Train: Liza and Henry. He's drawing.

Liza When you draw, what are you thinking?

Henry Nothing.

Liza Are you thinking about what you're drawing? Or are you drawing what you're thinking about?

Henry I'm in an alpha state.

Liza That's nice.

Henry Well, not now, obviously.

Liza Why not now?

Henry Not with you rabbiting on. You can't be in an alpha state with someone rabbiting on.

Liza Alright, I'll just sit here like a stone then, shall I? Like a lump of unformed clay at your side.

Henry Yes.

She makes a face at him.

Genius is only possible in a state of pure concentration.

Liza We're on a train.

Henry Genius can overcome trains. But not rabbiting. Winston Churchill sat next to a lady at dinner and didn't say a word for twenty minutes while he pondered Locke's theory of knowledge and probability.

Liza That's just rude. What's the point of being a genius if you can't hold a conversation?

Henry Rabbit rabbit rabbit. It's not rude. It's important.

Liza Who are you to say what's important and what's not important?

Henry I'm your beloved. And Archimedes got killed because he wouldn't look up from his book when the Romans came. 'If you don't stop working we'll kill you,' they said. But he didn't, did he, because he was right in the middle of an equation. Next thing he knows, there's a great big Roman knife through his heart. That's how I'd like to go.

Liza I'm sure it can be arranged.

Henry Oh, leave me alone.

Liza No. I won't. Human beings are not designed to be solitary.

>   *Liza brings out a banana from her bag and starts to eat it, hungrily. Henry stares at her.*

Do you want a banana?

Henry What did you say?

Liza Sorry.

Henry I've never had a banana in my life and I see no reason to start now.

Liza I'm sorry, I forgot.

9

Henry Go and get something else from the buffeteria, will you?

Liza You go.

Henry Wild whores wouldn't drag me down that corridor.

Liza Why not?

Henry It's better if you go. You'll be able to *chat*.

Liza If we weren't sitting on a train, I'd get off.

Henry If we weren't sitting on a train, you'd have nothing to get off.

Liza Oh, bugger off, you clapped-out old goat.

Liza goes. A few seconds later she returns.

What do you want?

Henry Cheese and pickle.

She looks expectant.

What? Please. Thank you. Sorry. What?

She holds her hand out. He digs in his pocket and gives her the money.

Oh, keep the change, why don't you? Twit.

Liza Twat.

Liza goes, leaving Henry alone.

Henry *Solitary.* Like a single goldfish in a bowl. Like a stone. Like a man on top of a mountain. Or like a diver at the bottom of the sea where no phones ring and there's nothing except the sound of your own breathing. Solitary. He wants to be alone. She's terrified of being alone. He has to go to the bathroom to be alone. She follows him everywhere. (It helps, to talk of myself in the third person. I'm not schizophrenic. But I don't know what I think until I hear what I say.) What would he do without her? Breathe. Yes. Become a genius? Scale the heights? Maybe. Plumb the depths? Probably. Starve? Oh yes. There is that. Companionship. Compromise. Caring. Sharing. Finding screwed-up tissues in your dressing gown. Wearing each other's wellies. Finishing each other's sentences. Losing all sense of individuality, autonomy and purpose. Or. Splendid isolation.

THREE

Inside, Joe stands behind Michelle, waiting for her to look up. She doesn't. She is busy reading a magazine and spooning ice cream out of a tub. There is the hum of a television in the background.

Michelle What?

Joe I'm hungry.

Michelle Alright, your best friend invites you out Saturday night, right, then blows you out at the last minute. Obviously she's got a better offer. Would you a) give her an earful; b) see if you can –

Joe Mum.

Michelle – get an invite too; or c) be relieved? A night in at last! (*She laughs mirthlessly.*) Oh please! You know what I mean. Okay. Forget that. Your neighbour – here's a good one – your neighbour comes round and asks you to turn your music down. (*Which prompts her to turn the television down with the remote control.*) Would you a) turn it up –

Joe There any food in the house?

Michelle – b) invite them to listen to it with you; or c) apologise and turn it down?

Joe Food, Mum.

Michelle I'd phone the police.

Joe For food?

Michelle d) Phone the police. The day he ever came round. Bloody mad dog man.

Joe Mum.

Michelle What?

Joe I'm starving.

Michelle Go on, then.

She offers him her tub of ice cream. He pushes it away.

Joe I hate coffee ice cream.

Michelle Why don't you go and have a cold shower? Look at you, all sweaty.

Joe I'm hungry. Not hot.

Michelle In the kitchen. I got a loaf in this morning and there's cheese in the thing.

Joe Fridge.

Michelle Yeah.

Joe I want a proper tea.

Michelle You what?

Joe Normal people eat meals. I want a proper *meal.*

Michelle What's the matter with you?

Joe Stew, casserole, chicken fricassee.

Michelle You gone mad?

Joe Steak and kidney pie. With peas.

Michelle It's too hot to *eat*.

Joe Dylan's mum makes her own pasta sauces.

Michelle Dylan's mum don't bloody work, does she?! Go and get yourself a Coke. You're just dehydrated. And fetch me one while you're at it, will ya?

He doesn't move. She carries on eating ice cream and focuses again on her magazine.

Hang on, here's one for you then. Your *girlfriend* says she's not going to give you anything for Valentine's Day because he doesn't believe in it. He – it says boyfriend, but you're not *gay*, are you, so. Do you a) Give your present to someone else?

Joe I haven't got a girlfriend, Mum.

Michelle Don't be stupid, I know you haven't got a girlfriend. But if you *had* a girlfriend –

Joe I don't want a girlfriend.

Michelle What, *ever*?

Joe I want sommat to eat.

Michelle *Are* you gay?

Joe No, Mum, I'm hungry.

Michelle 'Cos that cow at number nine keeps going on about how boys should always have a male in the household for, like, their sense of identity, like, someone to look up to, or else they won't know who they are. As if anyone would look up to *him*. As if *he* knew who he was, stupid arsehole.

Silence.

Joe Is he coming? At the weekend?

Michelle Bloody hope not.

Joe Only.

Michelle What?

Joe Only he left his electric razor behind.

Michelle Didn't know he had one.

Joe He might be missing it.

Michelle He knows where we are.

Joe But if I had his address, I could send it.

Michelle Well, we don't so we can't, so leave it. Right. Valentine's Day. Would you a) give your present to someone else; b) shame her by giving her your present anyway; or c) –

Joe I don't believe in Valentine's Day.

Michelle That's not in it, Joe. You got to go for a, b or c and then you add them all up at the end and that's what you are. I think I'm a b. Adaptive, flexible and patient. Oh, maybe not. Alright, an a, then. 'You want to right the wrongs in the world. Direct, confrontational, a fighter. You have a strong protective urge.' That's more like it. Yeah, anyone did anything to you I'd fuckin' brain 'em.

Joe is unmoved.

You gonna get that Coke then, or what?

Pause. He doesn't move.

No. Alright, I'll bloody get it myself then, shall I?

Joe doesn't answer. She makes an elaborate show of weariness as she gets up, and goes.
Joe turns the television up. He starts bouncing his ball on the spot but stops at the mention of Billy

14

Clyde. As he is drawn in, the light emanating from the TV reduces and intensifies on Joe's face.

TV Voice . . . The strike is set to continue, unless the union and representatives from the government are able to reach a solution before eight o'clock tonight. Police in the Midlands are launching an investigation into the disappearance of a twelve-year-old boy. Billy Clyde has been missing from his home now for twenty-four hours. (Hah! That stopped you in your tracks, didn't it?) He was last seen near his home in Quinford at approximately ten a.m. on August 3rd. A neighbour witnessed him cycling, unaccompanied, in the direction of the local skateboard park. (Actually, the skateboard park is in exactly the same direction as the garden centre and the kitchen shop, it's just that 'skateboard' and 'park' have got more sinister associations than shops or garden centres. All that graffiti and litter. Bit more salacious.) Police are appealing to anyone who may have seen Billy on that day or since, or to anyone who has any information which may lead to his whereabouts. (You, for example. Yes, you. You stand there feeling sorry for yourself, alone and misunderstood by your mum, who never stops eating ice cream and doesn't love you enough to cook you a proper meal, but look, my lad, something has actually happened there in your tedious suburban hell of a life and now's a chance for you to get *involved*. Mystery has entered the Estate. And, God forbid that I should be melodramatic about it, but your mate Billy may. Be. Dead. Or he might turn up in the morning wondering what all the fuss is about. But if it's tragedy on the doorstep, one thing is certain for you, my lad. Things will never be the same.) The weather tomorrow will be blustery with scattered showers. Low pressure over the North Atlantic . . .

The light fades on Joe till it becomes a spot. And disappears.

FOUR

Bill, in the garden. He is trying to balance a large pointed rock on top of another. The rock won't stay. He continues, with ineffable patience, to balance it . . .

FIVE

Train. Henry and Liza.

Henry Oh Liza, you shouldn't have left me. I've had a terrible time.

Liza I've had a terrible time. A man in the next carriage said there's a boy gone missing in Quinford.

Henry But we've just been through Quinford.

Liza Exactly. And police are appealing to anyone in the area who may have noticed anything or anyone suspicious. Which is us!

Henry We're not suspicious.

Liza We're in the area. We're in the area.

Henry Oh my God. The man!

Liza Which man?

Henry I knew he was dangerous. While you were gone. I was sitting here, minding my own business, when along comes this stranger and sits down beside me!

Liza Why?

Henry Exactly. Whole train to sit on, he sat so close he pinched my thigh.

Liza What did he want?

Henry Company, I suppose.

Liza Was he mad?

Henry As a bucket of maggots. We should tell the police.

Liza What, though?

Henry We have a suspect.

Liza But what did he do that was suspicious?

Henry I remember, I remember. He looked out of the window and he said – no, he got his glasses out first –

Liza Glasses?

Henry Yes! Glasses.

Liza Did he put them on?

Henry Of course he put them on. What else is he going to do with them? / Balance them on his middle finger? He put them on –

Liza Polish them? He might want to polish them.

Henry – and *then* he looked out the window.

Liza So he could see.

Henry Better. He wasn't blind. He wasn't a complete freak.

Liza Then what?

Henry And then he said, 'I hate the countryside, don't you? I hate the countryside. It's too big.'

Liza That's insane.

Henry That poor boy. Have they found the body yet?

Liza No, we mustn't jump to conclusions.

Henry Or is he lying somewhere in a ditch? All alone. Birds, hopping all over him, chirruping for help, and no one coming.

Liza Stop it, Henry. All we know is he's missing. And there's a nutter on the train.

Henry Call the police.

Liza But they'll want facts, details, evidence.

Henry Oh, I remember him perfectly. He had a face like a fruit bat, long hair, no nose to speak of –

Liza I mean something to connect him to the missing boy.

Henry Apart from the blood, you mean?

Liza What blood?

Henry He was covered in blood from head to foot, knife in hand, / left arm hanging limp by his side.

Liza No, Henry. He was not covered in blood. He didn't have a knife – stop it, that's enough!

Henry Shall I draw a picture of him? For the police to ponder?

Liza Oh yes, that's a good idea. Draw one of your lovely portraits. Do.

Henry searches his pockets.

Henry I can't find it.

Liza What?

Henry I can't find my pen.

Liza Left-hand pocket.

Henry I've looked.

Liza You must have left it behind.

Henry Don't be stupid. I've been using it.

Liza Well, what then?

Henry Oh no.

Liza What?

Henry You don't suppose?

Liza What?

Henry When I was looking out the window –

Liza What about it?

Henry I wasn't paying attention.

Liza To what?

Henry I don't believe it.

Liza Don't believe what?

Henry It must be . . .

Liza *Oh for the love of three oranges, what?*

Henry He's taken my pen.

Liza No!

Henry Well, where is it then?

Liza Just because you can't find it doesn't mean he stole it.

Henry You have no imagination sometimes. Logic can only take you from A to B. Imagination can take you anywhere.

Liza I don't want to go anywhere. I want to go to the coast.

Henry But not with a thieving murderer.

Liza Oh, this is awful. What are we going to do?

Henry You phone. I'll draw. Quick. Give me your pen.

Liza (*starts dialling her mobile*) Nasty thieving murdering pervert. Draw him, quick, draw him.

SIX

Police, interviewing Michelle, in her front room.

Michelle He had what I call a look about him. Big head, little shoulders. Older than his age. Posh shoes, can't remember the colour. But they was well off. Used to have carrots an' that in his packed lunch. I never knew his mum, they kept theirselves to theirselves mostly. Well, they can't have been here that long 'cos, I mean, we've only been here five years ourselves. Well, I have, I should say. I've been here seven years, if you count the first two.

Policeman Did you say you live alone, Mrs Rawlinson?

Michelle No.

Policeman You don't live alone?

Michelle I didn't say nothing about living alone.

Policeman So you do live alone?

Michelle Yeah.

Policeman Right.

He looks around the room, his gaze falling on a football nearby.

Michelle Apart from my son.

Policeman Your son?

Michelle Apart from my son, yeah.

Policeman You live apart from your son?

Michelle No. I live alone. Apart from him.

Pause.

Policeman And how old would he be?

Joe appears. The conversation continues as though he'd been there all along.

Joe Twelve.

Policeman And Billy was a mate of yours, was he?

Joe Yes.

Policeman When did you last see him, son?

Joe Thursday.

Policeman When exactly on Thursday?

Joe Coming-home time. We was kicking a can together. Him, me and Danny.

Policeman Did you notice anything unusual about him?

Joe No.

Policeman Nothing he said or did that might indicate he was unsettled in any way?

Joe Danny picked a fight with him. But there's nothing unusual about that. Danny picks fights with everyone.

Policeman Why?

Joe He's a muppet.

Policeman Billy?

Joe Danny.

Policeman Did Danny win the fight?

Joe He never wins the fight.

Policeman Can you tell me, in your own words, can you tell me exactly how the fight started?

Joe We're kicking the can on the pavement and Billly keeps kicking it onto the road. He can't help it, he's crap at football, but Danny thinks he's doing it on purpose so he trips him up and Billy lands on his ankle, twists it, gets up, clocks Danny and Danny, 'cos he's the fastest runner in school, Danny, he runs away, like shouting at Billy so he gets mad, only Billy doesn't get mad, he's not like that, he just ignores him and then we forgot about him, by the time we got to the Crescent which is where Billy lives, we forgot about Danny and that's that. I should have smashed his face in.

Policeman Do you think Billy was still angry with Danny when you left him?

Joe Nah.

Policeman Was Billy's foot alright when you left him?

Joe Yeah.

Policeman You said he twisted his foot?

Joe Yeah, but it was alright by then.

Policeman Which foot? Do you remember?

Joe That one.

Policeman The right?

Joe Yeah.

Policeman His right foot.

Joe You gonna ask me if he's right-footed?

Policeman No.

Joe So what do you reckon?

Policeman I'm sorry?

Joe What do you think's happened to Billy?

Policeman I'm not in a position to conjecture. We are, as I say, just trying to build up a profile by talking to as many people in the area as possible. Do you know whether your neighbour is in at all?

Michelle Yeah. He's always in.

Policeman Only the gentleman doesn't appear to be answering the door.

Michelle No, he doesn't answer his door.

Policeman Is he ill?

Michelle Not as far as I know.

Policeman And he lives alone?

Michelle Apart from his dogs.

Policeman Apart from his dogs?

Michelle Oh, here we go, apart from his dogs, yes. He lives alone.

Policeman How many dogs?

Michelle Seven.

Policeman That's a lot of dogs in a small house.

Michelle It's not that small. I mean, it's not as big as ours, obviously, because of the extension, but they're all quite spacious round here.

Policeman Have you been in it?

Michelle Fuck off! I mean sorry, officer, I wouldn't go in there if you paid me.

Policeman Do you not have a good relationship with your neighbour?

Michelle Relationship? I wouldn't call it that, no.

Policeman You're not on good terms?

Michelle It's not that. He keeps himself to himself, that's all.

Policeman You never talk to him?

Michelle Every few months, yeah. He talks. You listen. It's not like a conversation. But if you talk when he's not in the mood, he just runs away.

Policeman So when was the last time you spoke?

Michelle Palm Sunday.

Policeman I don't suppose you recall the content of your conversation?

Michelle He said, 'Your ash tree is eating up all my nutrients.'

Policeman You have a good memory, Mrs Rawlinson.

Michelle Well, if you only speak to someone once every two months you tend to remember the content, don't you?

Policeman And what did you say?

Michelle I cut it down.

Policeman Why?

Michelle He was right.

Policeman You didn't argue?

Michelle No. He's not stupid. Just weird.

SEVEN

Bill lets out a yelp of delight. He finally manages to balance one rock on top of the other. He stands back and admires his handiwork.

Bill Well well well indeed. Well well very well.

EIGHT

Train. Henry and Liza. Liza is on the phone.

Henry What if he walks past while you're on the phone to the rozzers?

Liza I'll pretend I'm talking to our niece.

Henry But she lives in Australia!

Liza He doesn't know that, does he?

Henry Alright. I could stand up and walk up and down the corridor, distract him. Or engage him in conversation.

Liza Do what you like. Only don't point at him and say, 'There's the murderer.' Yes, hello. Police. (*Pause.*) Alright, ambulance. (*Pause.*) Fireman, then. (*Pause.*) Well, what's available? (*Pause.*) We're stuck on a train with a man who we have reason to believe is a murderer. (*Pause.*) No, hang on hang on, I mean he's the man, we think he's the man who murdered the little boy from Quinford. (*Pause.*) Because he's just stolen my husband's pen! (*Pause.*) I don't know. (*to Henry*) What make was the pen?

Henry I can't remember. It was black.

Liza Black. (*to Henry*) Was it a fountain pen?

Henry Yes.

Liza Yes. (*Pause. To Henry*) Did it have a gold band at the top?

Henry Top and bottom.

Liza Yes, it had a gold band at the top and bottom. (*Pause. To Henry*) Did it have your name on it?

Henry No.

Liza This one's got your name on it.

Henry How does he know my name?

Liza How do you know his name? (*Pause.*) It's Henry. (*Pause. To Henry*) It's got your name on it.

Henry Is he taking the pup?

Liza Are you taking the pup? Hello? I said are you taking the pup? (*Pause.*) It's a polite word for piss. Well, you made me say it, officer, I had no intention of saying it –

> *They see the 'murderer' walk along the corridor. Henry gesticulates to Liza. She changes her tone abruptly.*

Henry Ssssssh, he's coming.

Liza Oh that's lovely, Carol, I'm so glad it arrived safely, yes, I certainly did, I knitted it myself from a pattern I had lying around – no, you know what I'm like, it'd be a jumper a day if I wasn't so busy with all the baking and the charities and the cat-rescuing – yes, didn't I tell you? We've got a new one called Beth, no, not *death*, nothing to do with death, or murder, although he's got very sharp claws. No, we haven't got mice, and anyway I wouldn't want to set the cat on them, I mean, obviously it's natural, I mean, no, killing isn't natural, I mean, if you're a cat, it's normal, it's not abnormal, like it would be if *we* went round killing mice, and throwing them in the air before biting their heads off, I mean I've done it with poison, which is probably just as bad, I really don't know because I've never actually seen a dying mouse, in the throes of death as it were, oh God, I mean how's your husband, whatsisname, Trevor?

> *Bill leaves. Henry makes gestures to Liza to signal that the coast is clear.*

Henry He's gone.

Liza Do you think he heard?

Henry Is he still there? Officer Dibble?

Liza Hello? Are you still there? (*Pause.*) He's gone as well.

Henry I'm not surprised. You twittering on about mice.

Liza Oh, what have I done?!

Henry It's alright. They'll have tracked the call and they'll have someone on their way within the hour.

Liza What will they do when they get here?

Henry They'll have him banged up. He'll be bound in chains of misery. Eating his own vomit and drinking his own urine, planning his escape with a teaspoon.

Liza We're alone! Abandoned! While a murderer runs rampant in the adjoining carriage – a murderer who is possibly even now incited to violence by the thoughts I accidentally put in his head of biting the heads off mice!

NINE

Inside: lounge. Michelle, watching the news. Joe, bouncing his ball around and getting in the way.

Michelle Not inside.

Joe What?

Michelle Outside.

Joe I can't see the telly outside.

Michelle Well, you can't play football inside.

Joe I'm not playing football.

Michelle Outside. Now.

Joe I might miss something.

Michelle There's nothing to miss.

Joe If I go outside –

Michelle I'll tell you. Alright? Anything happens, I'll tell you. Now go on, bugger off and play football.

Joe On my own?

Michelle Well, I'm not bloody playing, am I?

Joe Why not?

Michelle You think I got nothing better to do than mess about kicking balls? Only balls I want to kick are attached to your father.

Joe I don't want to play with myself.

Michelle Glad to hear it.

Joe Mum!

Silence. The TV draws them both back in.

Do you think he's dead?

Michelle Your dad? Bloody hope so.

Joe He could have just got lost.

Michelle Billy Clyde knew his way around. You can't get lost round here.

Joe I don't know what to do, Mum.

Michelle Put it this way. If Billy's dead, he's dead. If he's not, I don't want to think about it. His poor bloody mum. She'll be worrying herself sick, and them bastard newspaper men'll be camping out on her doorstep an' going through her dustbins. No, if I were her, I'd move. It'll never be the same now, whatever happens, they'll always think of her like that, like poor cow, even if they

don't say nothing it'll be there in their eyes. That Jean at
number six specially. Mooning about, pretending to
prune her stubby roses, you gotta watch yourself with
her, she catches you off-guard and before you know it
she's looking at you with her head on one side, going
(*sucking her teeth*) ooh an' aah and suddenly, bluurgh,
you're giving her the whole bloody life story. I know that
look, ever since your dad left they look at me like I just
got cancer since he buggered off, makes me want to
smack 'em in the muff, stupid housewives with their
husbands and their 'Oh, Jeff's very good at fixing things,
if ever you need a man' crap. They think your dad ever
fixed anything? He never even changed a ligtbulb, but oh,
they think, they must think the roof's fallen in now that
the pillar of the household's gone, taking his toolbox
with him, obviously, and you too young to be fixing
plugs yet. Jesus. None of them hardly pass the time of
day with me, now, all of a sudden I'm a community
project. Even that witch at number twenty-three always
wears her hair up in a turban 'cos she was a model for
Littlewood's in nineteen fifty-two, even she's started.
'How are you feeling, dear?' 'You're looking a bit tired,
love.' Excuse me! Fuck off. Five years ago was the last
time she spoke to me, whingeing on about the dog shit
outside her gate. Nothing to do with me, I said. We
haven't got a dog, have we? It's 'im next door as has 'em.
I can't stand the bastards. That shut her up. For a few
years anyway. Now she's sticking her nose in it again.
I'm telling you, there's nothing worse than sympathetic
looks from stupid people. And don't you go feeling sorry
for yourself neither, that's no good to you, me, him or
anyone's mum. You want to know what to do, you can
clear up your father's old tins at the bottom of the garden
'cos I'm not bloody going near them.

   Silence.

29

Joe I'll go and play football.

The sound of a football being kicked. Joe goes into the back yard. Bill is staring at his stones.
Joe kicks his ball. Bill hears the noise and ducks behind a plant, from where he watches Joe, unseen.
Joe continues kicking the ball, rhythmically. He loses control and accidentally boots it over the fence (the actual ball stays where it is. Joe's reaction suggests the arc of the imaginary ball as it goes out of bounds). He goes to climb over but, looking back at the house, he notices Bill's back door open and decides against it. He calls out instead.

Joe Mr T?

No answer.

Mr T!

He returns inside.
Bill emerges from his hiding place and retrieves a ball (actual). He rolls it along the ground, studying it intensely. He rolls it backwards and forwards, backwards and forwards. He marks the ball with a piece of mud and repeats the exercise. He laughs.
Joe reappears. He watches Bill for a while before speaking.

Can I have my ball back?

Bill Whoops.

Joe S'alright.

Bill Sorry.

Joe What you doing?

Bill Seeing if it works.

Joe Works?

Bill It does. It does work.

Joe Should do. It's new.

Bill It looks like it's going forwards, the curtate cycloid, but no, see, it's not. Not all of it. Like they say. Just like they say. (*He demonstrates, rolling the ball.*)

Joe You what?

Bill It's going at the same speed all the way round, you think it is, it looks like it is, but watch. See. Look. I put a dot. Here, watch the dot, look, see, see, the dot, how it goes. It goes backwards!

Joe I don't know what you're talking about, Mr T.

Bill It's a quarter turn, mmm, and yes, the length of it, turning, the quarter, here to here is shorter than, look, than here to here, so, the point, because for it has to go further here in the same length of time, mmm, the point must speed up! It must. It does. Look!

He demonstrates. They both watch intensely.

Joe Well, maybe you're pushing it faster.

Bill If I was a train, if I was a train, going the same speed, constant, mmm, the wheel, always, the wheel goes faster here, always, at the point of the longest quarter turn. See! And look how, look, look how it goes backwards! Some of it, always always always moving backwards as it goes forwards. At any point, at any time, always moving backwards as the train moves forwards!

Joe You mean, it looks like it is.

Bill No it is it is it is it is it is!

Joe Alright alright. Show me. Which bit?

Bill Watch. Look, see, slowly, catchee. (*He puts a mark on the ball with a pen and slowly rolls it.*)

Joe Oh yeah.

Bill See?

Joe Cool.

Bill Cool.

Bill stops the ball and hands it back.

You have your hollow orb back now.

Joe Cheers.

Bill Cheers.

Bill nods and smiles. Too much.

You you you are like a ballet dancer.

Joe Yeah, cheers.

Joe turns away abruptly and kicks the 'ball' against the wall with his back to Bill.

TEN

Train. Liza and Henry. Henry wakes up and looks out the window

Henry We've stopped!

Liza We stopped ages ago.

Henry Why didn't you tell me?

Liza You were asleep.

Henry Why?

Liza You were tired. It's late. We are creatures of circadian habit –

Henry Why has the train stopped?

There is an unintelligible train announcement.

What did he say?

Liza He said, 'We're stuck with a murderer on a train going nowhere.'

Henry You don't suppose he's killed himself?

Liza Or someone else?

Henry Or someone else.

Pause.

Liza No, we don't know, we don't even know if he's dead, the little boy.

Henry Of course he's dead. He'll have been abandoned by the forces of good by now. Throat cut. Limbs twisted. Clothes in disarray.

Suddenly she gets up. She makes to collect her stuff and leave.

What are you doing?

Liza I'm going.

Henry Where?

Liza Home.

Henry You can't. You can't leave me.

Liza Don't fucking tell me what I can and can't do. I'm going home.

Henry What about the murderer?

Liza He can make his own way back.

Pause.

Henry Oh my God. I've forgotten.

Liza What?

Henry Why I married you.

Liza Don't try and change the subject.

Henry You were talking and you said 'fucking', and I thought, 'It's not like you to say "fucking",' and I thought, 'Who is it like?' and I thought, 'Me!' and suddenly there was no difference between us and I forgot why on earth I married you.

Pause.

Liza Something to do with my eyes?

Henry No.

Liza My legs?

Henry No.

She sits down.

Liza My wit?

He shakes his head.

ELEVEN

Front room: Joe and Michelle. Joe, doing his homework. Michelle, eating ice cream out of the tub, and flicking through a magazine.

Joe Stupid damn stupid damn bloody bridges. I hate them!

Michelle Don't ask me, love, I didn't get maths.

Joe It's impossible. You can't get across each bridge only once. I've tried it every way, every single effing way there is, and you can't, you just can't.

Michelle And don't say the f-word.

Joe I didn't.

Michelle Yeah, well, don't.

Joe I'm going to ring Dad.

Michelle What for?

Joe He'll know.

Michelle No, he bloody well won't.

Joe He might.

Michelle He will not know.

Joe At least he'll listen.

Michelle I'm listening.

Joe He *might* know.

Michelle He never listens and he don't know nothing. What's got into you?

Joe I can't do it! (*He makes for the phone.*)

Michelle He won't be there. Don't you dare. He won't be in anyway, this time of day.

> *He picks the phone up and bangs it down. Silence. They stare at each other.*

I don't know how you can even think. I'm in shock.

> *Joe returns to his homework and sits, head in hands.*

Alright, come on then, bring it here.

> *He slaps it down in front of her. She picks it up and looks at it, unseeing.*

I'm not saying he's a complete moron, but he doesn't know fuck-all about anything. Maggie told me this is

35

what happens. Soon as they go, they start glorifying them. The dad becomes a hero. They forget. You haven't forgotten, have you? Just tell me you haven't forgotten.

Joe No.

Michelle What haven't you forgotten?

Joe Mum.

Michelle Oh, what am I supposed to be looking at, then?

Joe The bridges. You have to get across each bridge once. Only once.

Michelle That's easy. You go mn, mn, mn. No, da-dida-dida-didum. (*She stops, baffled by the puzzle.*) Why do you have to go across the bridges? Can't you just go round this bit?

Joe No.

Michelle That's stupid, then.

Joe It's impossible.

Silence.

Michelle You know what? We haven't had any tea, have we? Shall I make us a toastie? I'll go and make us a toastie.

Joe I'm not hungry.

Michelle Ham and cheese? Or just ham?

Joe I don't want one.

Michelle You sulking?

Joe No.

Michelle 'Cos if there's one thing I can't stand –

Joe Alright, alright, I'll have one.

Michelle I told you you were hungry.

She goes to the kitchen. Joe switches on the TV.

TV Voice . . . According to an official spokesman the government is not in a position to negotiate. 'We are not in a position to negotiate, and unless they honour their agreement we may be forced to take legal action.' (The truth is, since Billy's disappeared, you've got no one to ask, have you? He used to sit next to you in maths and now he's gone it seems like you don't know your arse from your hypoteneuse. And since your dad's upped and left you've got no one to shout at either. Forget your bridges a minute and concentrate on that evening, will you? There must be something to connect you to all this. Some little titbit of importance you can give them. Think about it. He'll have been abandoned by the forces of good by now. Limbs twisted. Throat cut. Clothes in disarray – Do you remember what it feels like to be important? To be at the centre of the universe? Two hands, you in the middle, Mum on one side, Dad on the other, swinging you up in the air. Or round and round, holding onto his hands for dear life while the G-force of it makes you want to throw up, but there's no question, all the same, there's no question of stopping. Do you remember his chin? The feel of his bristly chin on your face? This is long ago. Before the Ice Age. This is when you didn't even know your parents were divisible. When you thought they were one and the same, your mum and your dad, your dum and your mad, your dam and your mud, but *yours, all yours*. Some days, I've seen you, some days you put odd socks on, other days you put your shirt on inside out, don't you? Just to see if she'll notice. A little suburban fashion statement, otherwise known as a cry for help. I understand. If you're not bathed in natural warmth, just a moment in the limelight will do, and this could be yours, sonny, this could be your moment. (*Pause.*)

And the answer, for your information, is: you can't pass only once over each bridge. A traceable network can only have two odd vertices. This one has four, see, Joey my boy. It's impossible. You said it yourself.)

TWELVE

Clint appears with copies of The Big Issue *under his arm. He stands on a street corner and calls to passers by. Bill is drawn to him.*

Clint *Big Issue, Big Issue, Big Issue.* Don't be shy, don't walk by, don't turn a blind eye. *Big Issue, Big Issue, Big Issue.* Don't be shy, don't walk by, don't turn a blind eye. *Big Issue, Big Issue, Big Issue.* Don't be shy, don't walk by –

Bill approaches him

Bill If you look, you watch, you're standing in the wrong place here. Crossroads make people stop, yes, but they make people *cross*. Very cross. And there aren't as many: you, you stand on the island on the bend in the middle and you double your chances. So so so there.

Clint Thanks, mate, but this is my spot.

Bill You stand on a curve. People like a curve. Paradoxical curve. Snowflake curve. Parabolic curve.

Clint Doesn't matter where you stand, pal, it's the way you stand counts. Smile and the world smiles with you.

Bill You need dogs, big dogs, little dogs, any dogs – you got a dog?

Clint No, mate –

Bill You need a dog to get yourself a dog. A dog is a god is a dog is a god is a dog backwards, isn't it? Nothing they can't do. Dogs. Until the Industrial Rev – Rev – Revolution we used to eat them, didn't we? Now they're pets, there's nothing, no, a dog will provide you – there's nothing – only thing they can't do, a goat can but goats stink – can't mow the lawn. You got a lawn?

Clint No, mate, I haven't got a lawn.

Bill Course you haven't got a lawn. You haven't got a house! You haven't even got a room in a house, you haven't even got a bed, have you?! (*He laughs at his own joke.*) You cold? You want to borrow a dog. I got dogs. You can borrow a dog if you want, keep you warm, they keep you warm, dogs, cuddle up at night, they keep you warm, yes. Scott of the Antarctic would have done well to remember that. Minus 40 degrees. He might still be alive today if he'd thought a' that, eh. Cuddle your dog, don't eat it, mmmmm.

Clint Right.

Bill Your body temperature, drops below – well at minus ten your blood freezes, simple as that – you got to keep moving – mmmm mind you mind, Evans, he lay down and went to sleep in the snow twenty-four hours, snow kept him warm, woke up and he was alive. So but out here, you got to keep warm out here on the streets, oh yes, you got to look after yourself.

Clint Cheers, mate, cheers, yeah. Listen. I'll tell you how I look after meself. By selling these. I don't sell these, I don't eat. Dog or no dog. I gotta shift the lot of 'em. Alright?

Bill Go on then. Go on then.

Clint Don't be shy, don't walk by, don't turn a blind eye. *Big Issue*, *Big Issue*, *Big Issue*. Don't be shy, don't walk by, don't turn a blind eye. *Big Issue*, *Big Issue*, *Big Issue*. Don't be shy, don't walk by –

Bill looks around him, humming along to the rhythm of the chant. He inserts –

Come and buy!

– to the chant. Clint stops and fixes him with a look. Then continues. Bill does it again.

THIRTEEN

Train. Henry and Liza.

Liza My intellect?

Henry No.

Liza My kindness? Cooking? Cleaning?

Henry No.

Liza The way I smile?

Henry No.

Liza What then?

Henry Can't you remember?

Liza No.

Henry Oh God.

Liza Does it matter?

Henry Of course it matters. Without memory we're all *fish.*

Liza Memory doesn't make you human.

Henry It helps.

Liza Not necessarily. Memory is a crazy woman that hoards coloured rags and throws away food.

Henry Who said that?

Liza I've forgotten.

They sit in pensive silence.

FOURTEEN

*Backyard. Joe and Michelle are filling in a lottery form.
On the other side of the fence, in his garden, Bill is
weeding. He wears glasses.*

Michelle Five.

Joe Eight.

Michelle Thirteen.

Bill sticks his head over the fence.

Bill Twenty-one.

Michelle Oh blimey, Mr T.

Bill Thirty-four.

Michelle I've never seen you with glasses. Why are you
wearing glasses?

Bill Because it's Thursday. Five and eight is thirteen,
thirteen and eight is twenty-one, and thirteen is thirty-
four, fifty-five, eighty-nine, a hundred and forty-four, /
two hundred and thirty-three –

Michelle Hold on, hold on. We only need two more.

Joe What number'd you say?

Bill Each term is is is is the sum of the two preceding.
Twenty-one.

Michelle Twenty-one it is, then.

Joe And thirty-four.

Michelle You a numbers man then, Mr T?

Bill But every time you buy a card, ticket, number, the chances of you winning are less by one. One less. You got mmm more chance of winning if you *don't* buy one.

Michelle How's that?

Bill There's more probability of you finding one in the street.

Michelle Well, I'm sure you're quite right.

Bill Quite right.

Michelle And if we win, we'll cut you in, alright.

She goes inside.

Bill More probability that you will be hit by a car. More probability of finding two snowflakes the same. Mmmmm. More probability of two numbers being relatively prime.

Joe What's it called? That maths thing?

Bill Fibonacci sequence.

Bill suddenly gets up and marches towards Joe. He stops short by a cherry tree and grabs a branch.

This is nought. Say, this is leaf number nought. Take this, now which one, you say, which one is nought? Say this one.

Joe That one.

Bill This one, yes, yes, alright. Now, up, you go up, you go to the next one in line with it, your nought, and you count. Go on, count / until . . . yes, two-three-four-five.

Joe One-two-three-four-five.

Bill And again.

Joe One-two-three –

Bill Four-five –

Joe Five.

Bill Five, yes, you see, five! It's all there, you see, spiralling up. (*He gestures around his garden.*) Same with the lily. Same with the trillium. Same with the with the pear tree. You count. You see. You count. Don't get excited. Don't get excited. Don't get *excited*.

Joe counts the leaves with care.

Joe Five . . . five . . . they're all five!

Bill You see, you see, you see.

Joe I'm going to show Mum. This is cool.

He breaks off a stem of wild rose and ventures inside.

Bill (*to himself, and as if to cool himself down*) Cool. Cooool. Cooool.

FIFTEEN

Train. Henry is studying a cup.

Liza What are you doing?

Henry I'm trying to capture the light in the heart of darkness.

Liza Looks like you're copying a plastic cup to me.

Henry I don't copy. I draw.

Liza What happened to the murderer?

Henry I don't want to think about it any more.

Liza Why not?

Henry What's the point? No one's interested in what we think. What we think makes no difference.

Liza We have to think. What happens if it's not him? If he's just a lonely nutter? You should have talked to him. That would have made all the difference.

Henry Don't be ridiculous. He'll have a criminal record as long as your legs. A little chat about the countryside isn't going to prevent him from stealing a pen or sticking a knife into someone thirty-two times then chopping him up into little pieces and feeding him to the ducks, is it?

Liza We have a responsibility. What about that poor little boy? What about his parents, his friends? Have you no empathy?

Henry Buckets of the stuff. I just like to keep it to myself.

Liza It must be awful. Just imagine. To lose someone like that.

Henry Depends who it is.

Liza Oh shut up!

Henry You're assuming I mean you.

Liza Of course you mean me.

Henry There might be others.

Liza The fact that you find large numbers of people dispensable does nothing to mitigate your contempt for me.

Henry Can I just please finish my cup please?

Liza No. You're avoiding the issue. We are alone on a train with a murderer. We have to do *something*. You cannot hide behind paper cups and you haven't even eaten your sandwich yet. Here. Eat. Think.

SIXTEEN

Street corner. Bill, holding copies of the Big Issue. *Clint appears. He hands Bill a bottle of water. Bill drinks thirstily.*

Clint This bit of posh comes up to me, right, nice looking, bit old, forty-something, comes up to me, says 'I'm going for a coffee; would you like to join me?' I said, 'No thank you, I'm busy.' She gets the hump and walks off, straight past the café, she doesn't even go in it, she doesn't even *want* a coffee. Me, I already had two lattes and it's only ten a.m. and anyway I'm on shift till one, I just don't have time for that shit. And frankly, to be frank, I prefer it when they just come straight out and call you a stinking, gobshite parasite. Then we all know where we stand.

Bill On the pavement.

Clint On the pavement, yeah, mate. Very good. On the same pavement. My mate Jip, when I first met him, he comes up and asks if he can borrow a fiver. Now bear in mind I've never set eyes on the little sod before. I said to him, 'One, I don't do loans, two, can't you find anyone richer than me? I'm a fucking beggar for fuck's sake. Alright, so I'm not eating out of dustbins, but I'm not walking round Habitat eyeing up electric pepper grinders either, am I? Two pairs of jeans is all I got, and a jacket I nicked five years ago on the ferry to Calais, so just because I'm standing here, togged out, don't go taking me for granted you little shyster, what's your name anyway?' 'Jip,' he says, and starts to cry. Turns out he hasn't spoken to anyone for six and a half weeks. He doesn't want money, that's not what he's after, all he wants is a little bit of the milk of human and maybe a fag. But I won't let him have a fag, he's only twelve, the stupid runt, he's got the rest of his life to live for, hasn't he? So I look out for him now. I look out for him and he looks out for me.

Bill On the pavement.

Clint On the bloody pavement, mate, yeah. Where'd you live then, Bill?

Pause.

Bill Limestone pavements they form on English Irish Welshish limestone. Clints on top, grikes going down down to the bottom of the deep carboniferous limestone beds three hundred and fifty million years ago is when it all started.

Clint You're not from round here, then?

Bill What?

Clint Where you come from?

Bill Come from?

Clint Never mind.

Silence.

You want a latte?

Bill What?

Clint One o'clock. Coffee break.

He goes.

Bill Shall I follow? (*Pause.*) I'll follow.

SEVENTEEN

Joe, sits in his back yard, listening to music on his headphones, trying to do his homework.

Michelle, lying next to him, wears a bikini. She's drinking beer and listening to music on her headphones.

Bill appears in his garden. He peers over the fence at them, friendly. Joe doesn't notice him at first.

Bill Hello.

Michelle Oh, hello.

Bill Hello.

Michelle We haven't seen you for ages, Mr T. What've you been up to?

Bill I've been masturbating quite a bit.

She chokes on her beer but he continues, unaware.

And I went down the skip skip skip last week, found an old desk, I been working on it, for the dogs, they like a little den, little hideout. Hacking and sawing, hacking and sawing.

Michelle Jesus Christ.

She walks up to Joe and lifts his headphones for a moment.

Did you hear that?

Joe What?

Michelle Good.

Joe What?

Michelle Keep 'em on.

She replaces his headphones and goes inside. Joe takes them off.

47

Joe Mr T. Can you – could you help me with my homework?

Bill No.

Joe You could do it, easy. I can't do any of it.

Bill No, no, no, thank you.

Joe Oh go on.

Bill You go on.

Joe Please.

Bill I'm a s – s – s – s –

Joe I can't do it on my own.

Bill I'm a silly fat boy with ideas above my-my-my-my – (*He stops abruptly, having forgotten the word.*) – airport.

Joe You're not fat, Mr T.

Bill You're not fat, Mr T

Joe You're not. Or silly.

Bill *You.*

Joe I'm useless.

Bill You're . . .

Joe What?

Bill Mmm.

   Pause.

Joe Will you do it, then?

Bill No.

Joe Oh please, Mr T.

Bill I hate school.

Joe You don't have to go to school. I just want you to help me with this.

Bill Everyone has to go to school, my lad, you can't stay at home getting under my feet just because you don't like it, dragging your fat arse around the house. What do I want with you here? What do I want with you?!

Silence.

Joe Are you alright?

Bill You're alright. You're alright. Look.

Joe What?

He reaches out to trace the contours of Joe's arm.

Bill Beauty.

His hand follows a vein all the way up to his bicep and hovers there.

Full.

He gasps, stares at it, then retracts his hand. There is a momentary awkwardness between them. Joe breaks it.

Joe There's this boy called Billy, right. He was my friend. Billy Clyde. And he's disappeared. / No one knows what's –

Bill Yes, yes, yes.

Joe – happened to him, I mean everyone *thinks* they know but no one's saying, and I feel like I should know something, because there's a connection between us, I mean, he was my friend and I keep thinking, I can't help thinking, it could have been me. She'd notice me, if I went missing, wouldn't she? And what if he's alright? What if he's alright and he's just having a laugh, it's all a big wind-up and everyone's going on about Billy this, Billy that, and maybe he's just sitting somewhere, having a cheese roll and watching it all on telly.

Bill Billy Clyde. Born 3rd June 1992. Disappeared, morning of the 3rd August. Last seen last seen last seen at 9.45 wearing pale-blue shirt and shorts, dark-blue, denim, cut-off, yes, and a Spiderman watch.

Joe How come you know all that?

Bill Police.

Joe They came to see you?

Bill (*mimicking Joe*) They came to see you?

Joe Yeah, but I knew him. He was my friend.

Bill 'Conducting enquiries in the neighbourhood hood.'

Joe But how come you remember all that?

Bill I remember everything.

Joe What else do you remember?

Bill I remember everything.

Michelle appears in the doorway and shouts to Joe.

Michelle Get inside here, Joe Rawlinson!

Joe What?

Michelle Now!

Joe Why?

Michelle Because I say so.

Joe Mum.

Michelle I'm not asking again.

Joe (*to Bill as he hands him his book*) Here. Just have a look at it, will you? Go on. Just a little look.

Joe goes inside.

Bill I'm sitting on a bench in a park. I'm seven. On a park bench. Yes. Cold bum. A woman next to me. It's my mum, I think. I think it's my mum. I'm seven and I've got a snot snot snotty nose. She hasn't got a tissue. I certainly haven't got a tissue, have I?! Cheeky! I wipe it on my sleeve, my nose, and she cuffs me on the head, Mum does. Nicely. Cuff. Like that. Mmmm. Then gets up. Forages about in the bushes, comes back, she comes back with a dock-leaf the size of a pillow, makes me blow into it. And then and then, I'm sure it's my mum, she cuddles me. Bum's still cold. She cuddles me. Oh yes, I remember that. Can't forget that. I remember that.

EIGHTEEN

Train. Henry eating his sandwich. Silence. Suddenly Henry puts his sandwich down and pushes it away from him in disgust.

Henry Oh God, no.

Liza What?

Henry I can feel it coming.

Liza What is it?

Henry No, no, I can't bear it.

Liza What's happened?

Henry It's happening.

Liza It's okay, it's alright. It'll pass, remember it'll pass.

Henry No, it will never pass.

Liza It will.

Henry Don't go.

Liza Hold on.

Henry To what? To what?

Liza To me.

He does.

Henry It's closing in. There's no light. I can't.

Liza Go back, you can go back to the beginning.

Henry No-no-no-no.

Liza How did it start?

Henry I was just sitting here.

Liza And then?

Henry And then.

Liza Was it something I said?

Henry No.

Liza What then?

Henry Something I saw.

Liza Out the window?

Henry No!

Liza Can you see it now?

Henry Yes!

Liza What is it?

Henry That.

He points at his sandwich.

Liza A sandwich.

Henry No. *That.*

Liza The lettuce.

Henry Disgusting.

Liza It's gone bad.

Henry A disgusting lettuce leaf.

Liza Yes, yes, I see.

Henry I touched it. And then and then . . .

Liza And then?

Henry Then it was the brains of a child, poor dead child whose head is split open and squashed, like a water melon, seeds and red-fruit flesh spilling out onto the pavement and the pavement's turned into a minefield with a man on every corner handing out parking fines and ripping the heads off chickens / and the women are starving themselves until their bones stick through their skin like half-eaten trout.

Liza Sssh, shshhsh, it's alright, it's okay, it's okay.

Henry It's not okay. You made me think. You made me think terrible things.

Liza Thinking's not a crime.

Henry It is. It is. I dream of your death at least once a week.

Liza But it doesn't make any difference, does it? I'm still here.

Henry But if my imagination can do no harm, how can it do any good?

Pause.

Liza Give me the leaf.

Henry What?

Liza Give me the lettuce leaf.

Henry looks at the sandwich but doesn't move. Liza opens it slowly, carefully, and takes out the offending

53

lettuce leaf. Henry gasps. Liza holds it up for Henry to see.

Lettuce. Avaunt.

She throws it out the window. Then finds a fresh one from inside the sandwich and offers it to him.

Here. It's new. A new leaf.

Henry Do I have to turn it over?

Liza No, just eat it.

He does. It makes a crunchy sound.

Better?

He is unable to speak. But his breathing slows down and he nods.

NINETEEN

Inside. Joe stands in front of the television, transfixed. Michelle is tidying up like a whirlwind, picking up papers, moving them around, or just throwing them away.

TV Voice . . . But police have reason to believe that whoever has abducted Billy Clyde may still be at large in the area. They are appealing to anyone who might have noticed anything unusual. (Truth is, they haven't a clue what they're looking for, and saying things like that helps to raise the general level of paranoia which has the concomitant effect of lowering the statistical crime rate. For a couple of days anyway. People don't go out unless they have to really. Simple as that. Anyway, you might remember something. Something banal, like if you were late coming back from work that day, maybe you were stuck in a traffic jam, and so, to avoid that traffic jam, you might have done a U-turn to go another way, and in doing so you might have gone straight into the path of an angry car, with a man in it, waving his fist, as well he might and, if you try hard enough, you can remember his face and the colour of the car. An impatient man in a car, always a bad sign. Or you might have seen a young boy, out of the corner of your eye, running for his life, chased by a man with a large machete knife, perhaps? Or you might, as if in a dream, have been distracted by the incongruous sight of a large rucksack on a small boy, the boy looking too small for the rucksack, the rucksack looking too heavy for the boy, as he boarded a bus and, looking behind him for the last time, tripped on the step and fell. Thing is, Joey, and I hope you're paying attention now, it's not every month, is it, that you lose your mate and your dad. Bring one back, the other one might follow, eh.)

The TV fades to silence. Joe looks to Michelle and back to the telly again.

Joe Did you hear that?

Michelle Mm?

Joe Did you hear what he said?

Michelle They found him?

Joe No.

Michelle What then?

Joe It's just –

Michelle Turn it off, will you, it's giving me a headache.

Joe The man –

Michelle What man?

Joe The newsman.

55

Michelle Gavin.

Joe Do you know him?

Michelle Gavin Donaldson. No, course I don't.

Joe The way he talks. He seems – I dunno.

Michelle Welsh.

Joe No.

Michelle He is, he's Welsh.

Joe No. *Friendly.*

Michelle The Welsh *can* be friendly.

Joe As if he knows me.

Joe is sitting in the spot she wants to tidy next. She shoos him away.

Michelle Look. I'm trying to tidy up round here.

Joe gets up and looks out into the garden.

Joe We could eat outside. It's sunny.

Michelle Doesn't make any difference. I've still got to tidy up, haven't I?

Joe If Dad was here –

Michelle Oh, don't start.

Joe No, if Dad was here –

Michelle Don't even start. Alright?

Joe Alright.

Michelle What? 'If Dad was here' what?

Joe He might have done us a barbecue tonight.

Michelle Yeah. And he'd have burnt the sausages. And then he'd have cursed at me and thrown them on the floor and gone out the house, he'd have slammed the door and gone off down the King's Head leaving us to a bowl of chilli pepper sauce and chips and he'd have come home three o'clock in the morning, smelling of sick.

Pause.

Joe (*quietly*) But he'd have come home.

Michelle Then he'd have got up, in time for work, he'd still have got up, got himself dressed, and he'd have come downstairs with a face like a sheep's arse, he'd have sat hisself down and I'd have made his breakfast, wouldn't I, I'd have done it all, I'd have done it *happily* but for one word, that one little word.

Joe Sorry.

Michelle No good you saying it for him. It's no good *you* saying it.

Silence. Upset now, Michelle busies herself again with her manic tidying.

Joe Mr T says there are patterns, everywhere around you, there are patterns in the leaves, in the flowers, in the trees, the sky, everything, that the world has patterns you can't even *see* with your naked eye even, and that sometimes those patterns are broken but that's a pattern too, the breaking of the pattern.

Michelle He's a bloody nutter.

Joe He's not a bloody nutter. I like him.

Michelle You wanna watch him.

Joe He knows interesting facts. About the planet.

Michelle What's that got to do with the facts? What's that got to do with the facts of life?

Joe What facts?

Michelle Food. Money. Roof. Head.

Joe You're a bloody nutter.

Michelle How dare you?

Joe Sorry.

Michelle I gave you *birth*, how dare you call me that?

Joe I didn't mean it.

Michelle I am not a bloody nutter.

Joe I'm sorry.

Michelle I might be a bloody cow. But I'm not a nutter.

Joe No, Mum, you're not a cow.

Michelle A bloody cow, sucked dry, teats shrivelled, arse branded. A number. Just a bloody number.

Joe He's good with numbers too.

Michelle Oh, that's alright, then. Go on, off you go, take your calculator round there then, go on, swapping numbers and drawing patterns, stop him staring out the window all day, God only knows what he does in there, him and his bloody dogs that never bark. They're not even noisy. What are they doing? Are they drugged? Have they got tongues? They never bark. It's not natural. Not even when the phone rings. Well, he hasn't got a phone, has he? Hasn't even got a phone. Last time I saw anyone near his front door was a smelly-looking man, he didn't even get invited in. There were words. But he didn't go in. Stood out on the doorstep long after the nutter shut the door and it was raining. I would have invited him in, only why should I? Last time I had a member of the male species cross my threshold was that bloke who turned up from electricity. You telling me – I said – you telling me they've got to send a little man round with a little machine like that – you haven't got no centralised thingy? He said if I didn't let him in he'd just do an estimate based on the last time in which case why'd he knock on the door in the first place if he didn't *need* to? He had wavy black hair and nice brown eyes, but he wasn't English.

Joe We could ask him round.

Michelle Who?

Joe Mr T.

Michelle Why?

Joe We could have a barbecue and ask him round. I could do it. I could do the meat.

Michelle What for?

Joe My birthday.

Michelle You what?

Joe Why not?

Michelle It's not your birthday.

Joe Yes it is.

Michelle When?

Joe Today.

Michelle Fuck off, it's not today.

Joe Friday.

Michelle Oh God, it is an' all.

Joe We could get some tinnies in.

Michelle Listen to him. Tinnies! Who do you think you are?!

Joe Go on.

Michelle Who do you think I am?

Joe Just a little party.

Michelle What, you, me and the nutter?

Joe We could ask someone else. So he won't feel shy.

Michelle Who the bloody else is gonna want to come and listen to a talking calculator?

Joe Darrell?

Michelle I'm not having Darrell in the house after last time.

Joe Nan.

Michelle We're not on speaking terms, remember?

Joe What about – what about Sean, then?

Michelle Look. It's your birthday, Joe. If you want to invite all the delinquents in the world over, that's fine. But don't expect me to run around baking cakes and making jelly.

Joe We could just do sausages. I don't mind.

Pause.

Michelle He wouldn't come.

Joe He will.

Michelle Bet you five quid.

Joe I haven't got five quid.

Michelle You will have.

Joe When?

Michelle On your birthday.

Joe Go on then.

They shake hands.

Michelle But I'm not going to ask him. You'll have to.

Joe I will.

Michelle If he does come, mind, I'm not talking to him.

Joe I'll ask him.

TWENTY

Train. Henry and Liza.

Liza How long have we been here?

Henry Two and a half weeks.

Liza Where the hell are we, anyway?

Henry We're stuck between omniscience and impotence. We believe in statistics but we dream of God. We're in two places at once and nowhere at all.

Liza looks at him with weary patience: he cranes his neck to see out the window.

We're the other side of Hinton Coombe.

Liza Abandoned and alone.

Henry We can't be alone. As long as we're together we can't be alone, can we?! Oh God, I'm bored.

Liza I'm bored and I'm cold and I'm tired.

Henry You're not old. You just look it. / It's the liver-spots.

Liza I didn't say old. I said cold.

Henry That's it! That's it!

Liza What?

Henry I remember why I married you.

Liza Let's hear it then.

Henry Because you were the first woman I met –

Liza Is that it?

Henry Who wouldn't leave me alone.

Liza Dear Henry. No, I wouldn't do that.

Henry No. You wouldn't, would you?

Liza Never.

Henry My heart was broken. And you came along.

Liza And mended it.

Henry You did.

Liza It's still mending.

Henry It is.

Liza I love you, dear Henry.

Henry Dear Liza. Dear Liza.

Liza And I'll never leave you.

Henry *Alone.*

Liza Oh look! Listen! Did you feel that? We're moving.

Henry We're not?

Liza We are. Look out the window!

Henry Oh, thank God.

He stands up to see better out the window.

Liza Don't stand up!

Henry Why not? I'm happy.

Liza You might interfere with its trajectory.

Henry It's a train, not a boat.

Liza I don't want to stand up.

Henry You don't have to.

TWENTY-ONE

Back yard. Michelle, Joe and Bill. Michelle is getting drunk. She has an old calendar with which she and Joe are testing Bill.

Michelle July 3rd.

Bill Friday.

Michelle Friday.

Joe September 6th.

Bill Tuesday.

Michelle Jesus Christ, my lord. Alright, how about . . . April Fool's Day?

Bill looks at her, perplexed.

Bill Who?

Joe The first. April the first.

Bill Sunday.

Michelle No, Saturday!

Bill Sunday.

Joe No, it's Sunday.

Michelle Oh yeah, I'm looking at the wrong S.

Bill Who's a fool?

Michelle I am, Mr T. Here, how about my birthday. Same year, June 29th?

Bill Friday.

Michelle How do you know? How do you know it was a Friday?

Bill Because I went to the café on Thursday.

Michelle This is years ago.

Bill And I had two egg and chips.

Michelle You're unbelievable, Mr T. You should be on the telly.

Bill I wouldn't fit.

Michelle No, someone like you, you'd be really useful down the shop. They're always asking what rota I did beginning of the month, and I can't remember can I? Joy, of course, she writes everything down, but then she hasn't got any dependents, has she? I should bring you along. Be nice to have you on my side.

Bill I'm on your side, I'm on your side.

Michelle You like it? You never been in our garden before, have you?

Bill No.

Michelle You don't like it?

Bill No.

Michelle Oh.

Bill I like lemonade. There are no flowers. I like lemonade. (*He gulps it down.*)

Michelle Yeah, well it's for Joe, really, innit. And his football. (*She notices he's drunk most of the lemonade down in one go.*) Bloody hell, that's it then, innit.

Joe You've got a beautiful garden, Mr T.

Bill I have.

Michelle Yes, you have. Because you've got time, haven't you? I haven't got time. You're right. Ours is a tip.

Joe I mowed it yesterday.

Michelle Did ya?

Joe You know I did.

Michelle Don't ask me to remember what happened yesterday. This household, I don't know whether I'm coming or going half the time. Well, I know when I'm *coming*, obviously. You probably know when I'm coming, walls are that thin.

Joe Mum!

Michelle Yeah, he mowed it yesterday, my little man. It's his birthday today, you know.

Joe He knows, Mum. He knows it's my birthday.

Bill Happy birthday.

Joe Yeah, thanks.

Bill Happy birthday.

Joe Cheers.

Bill Did it hurt?

Michelle What?

Bill Giving birth.

Michelle Bloody hell. Yes, as a matter of fact. 'Just like passing a melon,' they say. Fuck melons. Melons are a piece of cake. It's more like trying to get a television out.

Bill I remember.

Joe You what?

Bill Being born.

Michelle Or like pushing out an open umbrella.

Joe You remember being born?

Bill I remember.

Joe Jesus. He remembers being born.

Michelle Get off it. Go on then, don't tell me it's all trumpets and angels.

Joe What's it like?

Bill Nice squash.

Michelle Squashed. I should cocoa.

Bill Any more lemonade?

Joe No. Being born. What's it feel like?

Bill Lemonade squash.

Michelle He wants some more.

Joe We got any more?

Michelle Here's a quid. Go down the corner.

Joe Two quid and I'll get us another packet of subs.

Michelle doesn't hear. Assuming he's gone, she turns to Bill, conspiratorially.

Michelle When he was born, Joey, when he was born, right – (*She becomes aware of Joe at her shoulder.*) You still here?

Joe What?

Michelle You gonna get our guest some more of his chosen?

Joe What happened when I was born?

Michelle It's between me and Mr T.

Joe It was my birth.

Michelle No, your birth*day*. *My* birth.

Joe Go on, then. What happened?

Michelle I was going to tell you when you're older.

Joe I am older.

Michelle No, *older.*

Joe I'm thirteen. Today.

Michelle I mean grown up.

Joe What happened when I was born that you can't tell it me now?

Bill's disturbed. He starts to hum, one single note, to block out the sound.

Michelle Oh God. Now look what you've done.

Joe What? Am I adopted? What?

Michelle No, of course you're not, you stupid git. Look at your ears.

Joe Sorry, Mr T. It's alright, it's alright.

Michelle What's wrong with him?

Joe He's upset.

Michelle tries to stroke his arm.

Michelle Hey. Mr T. It's alright.

Joe Don't touch him.

Michelle Why not?

Joe He doesn't like it.

Michelle How do you know?

Joe I just don't think he'll like it.

Michelle Why not?

Joe We're not arguing now, Mr T. It's alright.

Michelle Yes we are. Why can't I touch him?

Joe Do you think we should hum, too?

Michelle I'm not bloody humming.

Joe hums. After a while Bill stops abruptly and looks at Joe.

Bill Why you humming?

Joe shrugs.

Michelle It's his birthday. He's happy.

Bill I know I know I know.

Michelle Alright.

Joe I still want to know, Mum.

Michelle Alright. Okay. You know I always told you how you came out in the bath?

Joe Yeah.

Michelle Well, you didn't.

Joe What then?

Michelle You were born in the toilet.

Joe Toilet?

Michelle You just came out. I was sitting on the toilet, minding my own business after days of agony, and you popped out. We nearly lost you down the U-bend.

Joe starts to laugh. After a while Bill joins in.

Joe The toilet –

Michelle You were fine. But I was shaking like a bloody road drill and so was the midwife. We stood there, me and her, passing you back and forwards, didn't know what to do with you – what you laughing for, you prat?

Joe Why did you tell me I was born in the bath?

Michelle I thought you'd prefer it to the toilet.

Joe I don't care. I don't mind where I was born. It's nothing to do with me, is it?

Michelle I thought it might be a stigma.

Joe Nah.

Bill Stigma.

Joe No. A stigma is something that sticks to you.

Bill A blot.

Joe When it's not true.

Bill Smirch.

Joe I couldn't care less if I was born down the toilet.

Bill Slur.

Joe Long as I wasn't brought up in it.

Michelle Lemonade, Mr T?

Bill Shame.

Michelle D'you want to get some more lemonade for your guest?

Joe Yeah, gotta visit my birthplace first, though.

Joe goes. Bill looks deeply into his empty glass. Silence.

Michelle Done any more masturbating lately, Mr T?

Bill No. Too busy planting.

Michelle Sewing your seed. Well it's better than wasting it.

Bill Potatoes, carrots, parsnips. Root crops. It's a full moon tomorrow night.

Michelle Quite the romantic, aren't you?

Bill It's a question of moisture. There's more m-m-m-moisture in the soil. The gravitational pull on the earth, it makes two tidal bulges it does and so the plants, they absorb more water. Tomorrow night. The moon will be full.

Michelle Well, that's something to look forward to.

Bill Not all plants, though. Flowers favour temperature. But I have a lot of seeds. I can give you some seeds.

Michelle Steady now.

Bill But you mustn't put them in the ground.

Michelle Where should I put them?

Bill Not yet. No. They're for later.

Michelle Course they are. You ever had a girlfriend, Mr T?

Bill I've got a friend.

Michelle Oh?

Bill I don't think he likes me, though.

Michelle I like you. I think you're alright.

Bill I like lemonade.

Michelle I reckon you're a virgin, in't ya?

Bill Lemonade's what I like.

Michelle Here. You wanna come and park your clever bum down next to my stupid arse, Mr T?

Pause. It takes a while for the question to register.

Bill No!

Michelle How about if I come to your level, then? How's about that then?

She stands up and faces him. Taking his hands, she places them gently on her breasts.

What do you reckon?

Bill Oh.

Michelle Nice?

Bill Soft. Like a bad apple.

Michelle Have a feel. Go on.

Bill Big. Bad. Grapefruits.

Michelle Mmm.

Bill Squish. Squash. Squish. Squash.

Joe enters the garden.

Joe You forgot to give me the extra quid.

Bill Squish.

Joe stands rooted to the spot. Michelle tries to extricate herself from Bill.

Michelle That's enough now.

Bill Squash.

Joe What's going on?

Bill Squish.

Michelle Off. Come on.

Bill Squash.

Joe What's he doing?

Bill Squish squash squish squash squish.

Michelle Get off, go on, off. Stop it.

Bill Squash!

Michelle Ow! Bloody hell! That's enough.

Michelle pushes Bill off.

Joe Bloody get off her!

Michelle That hurt.

Joe What do you think you're doing? What's he think he's playing at?

Michelle Leave it. He didn't mean it.

Joe Leave her alone.

Bill Leave her alone.

Joe Shut up.

Bill Shut up.

Joe *Shut up.*

Bill *Shut up.*

Michelle Leave it, Joe.

Joe (*to Bill*) Get out!

Bill Out!

Joe Get out of my garden.

Bill Shut up.

Joe Go on. OUT!

Bill OUT!

Joe OUT!

Bill looks at Joe, stunned.

Go.

Bill turns and walks out. Silence.

Michelle Poor thing.

Joe No.

Michelle He's just a bit confused. D'you get that lemonade?

Joe Mum.

Michelle Only I'm parched.

Joe I haven't got any cash. That's why I came back.

Michelle Here.

Joe Mum.

Michelle Big bottle, alright. I don't want none of those tins make it taste all tinny.

Joe *Mum.*

Michelle What?

Joe What did he . . . did you . . . what . . . ?

Michelle *What?*

Silence.

Joe I didn't think you liked lemonade.

Michelle Or Coke. Whatever. It's your birthday.

Joe I'm not thirsty.

Michelle Coke then. And a couple of Kit-Kats. 'Kay?

Joe 'Kay.

Michelle It's your birthday. Keep the change.

He goes. She looks down at herself. Cups her hands over her breasts, then folds her arms across her body, and hugs herself, hard, and starts to rock to and fro.

TWENTY-TWO

Train. Henry and Liza.

Henry Huh! My pen!

Liza What about it?

Henry It is, it's my pen!

Liza Oh, you prat.

Henry In my inside pocket.

Liza I don't believe it.

Henry It was there all along! My pen, my beautiful pen.

Henry clasps the pen to him and sits down.

Liza What are we going to tell him?

Henry Who?

Liza 'The murderer'.

Henry You have to stop calling him that, for a start.

Liza I've been giving him terrible looks. We have to explain.

Henry What, that we had him down as a psychopath and thief?

Liza I told you there might be an element of doubt.

Henry I told you we should have stayed out of it.

Liza You said nothing of the sort. You were the one who wanted him arraigned before the judge and submitted to public disembowelment.

Henry You can go if you want. I'm staying here.

Liza I'll take him the picture you did of him. He'll like that.

Henry No, you can't. It's got a reward sign at the bottom.

Liza Well draw another one and make him look nicer. I'll come back for it.

She goes.

TWENTY-THREE

Joe hurtles out of his house into the back yard. He kicks his ball angrily against the wall. Disturbed by the noise, Bill ventures out into his garden. He is frightened.

Bill Please. It's too hard. Please.

Joe kicks the ball even harder.

No, please. You mustn't. Stop. You have to stop.

Joe kicks the ball high up in the air and away. They both follow the arc of the ball with their eyes. It's clearly not coming back. Silence.

Oh dear.

Joe starts to laugh. And then cry.

No, oh no, you mustn't cry. You mustn't cry. Don't you cry. STOP! Don't you dare cry. YOU MUSTN'T CRY.

Surprised, Joe stops crying.

Joe I see you sometimes, Mr T, in the middle of the night, I see you. In your garden.

Pause.

Bill Yes.

Joe What are you doing?

Bill What are *you* doing?

Joe Just watching.

Bill Watching me?

Joe Yes.

Bill Planting.

Joe Planting what?

Bill By the light, by the light of the silvery moon the potatoes grow better, stronger, quicker, don't they? You plant them by the light of the full moon.

Silence.

Joe Billy's dead.

Bill No, I'm not.

Joe They found him by the skip.

Bill What skip? I know the skip. I go down the skip. I haven't seen no one by the skip.

Joe He was in the bushes near by.

Bill Billy.

Joe Three weeks he's been there.

Bill Your friend Billy.

Joe Both his legs were broken.

Bill I'm your friend Billy.

Joe My friend Billy is *dead*. Oh, I don't want to talk about it.

Bill (*mimicking*) Oh, I don't want to talk about it.

Joe I don't want –

Bill I don't want –

Joe Don't.

Bill Don't.

Joe Stop it.

Bill Stop it.

Joe Please.

Bill Please.

Joe Will you shut up? Jesus.

Bill starts to hum. He becomes absorbed in studying the head of a sunflower and stops.

If I had a bike I might have gone with him. And if I'd gone with him it wouldn't have happened. I haven't got a bike, though, have I? He never even came to my house. Why would he? No one else does. He probably didn't even like me. I only went round his once, when I cut my chin open, and no one was even there even, so we had that in common, but I reckon he didn't mind his mum never being there, I reckon he liked being on his own. I don't. I hate it. I bloody hate it.

Bill You're not on your own. She's there. Where's Mr –?

Joe What?

Bill Haven't seen him. We haven't seen him, have we, Mr Rawlinson?

Joe He's left.

Bill You're right.

Joe You what?

Bill He's left, you're right, she's gone. He's left, she's right, you're gone. He's gone, she's right, you're left. When's he coming back, then?

Joe He's not coming back.

Bill That's it, then. Have to get get get another one. She'll get another one. She with her skirts and and her legs and her looks and her lips and her big big big balloons.

Joe SHUT UP!

Bill freezes, as if expecting to be hit.

What's the matter with you?

Bill He's dead.

Joe No! He's not dead. *Billy's* dead. My dad –

Bill Is not coming back.

Joe No.

Bill Never never ever never?

Joe No. (*Pause.*) Except to see me.

Bill You're still here.

Joe He's busy at the moment.

Bill You're still here. When?

Joe What?

Bill When will he visit?

Joe I don't know. He can't plan ahead, his job. He'll more likely just turn up.

Bill Something always does. Something always does.

Joe It's his job. He doesn't know what he's doing till he's doing it. He'll call in the morning. He'll let me know on the morning of the day he comes. Last minute.

78

Bill Oh no.

Joe What?

Bill 'You will not know which day the exam will happen until you are told of it on the morning of the day it will happen.' So. The exam, it cannot be on Friday because it is the last day it could be given and you could deduce this on Thursday, see, if you had not had it yet. So, if not Friday, Thursday is the last possible day, but it can't be, can it, because, by Wednesday you would know Thursday and Friday are left and since Friday is out, remember, on Wednesday you would know ahead of time it would be Thursday, and this you are not supposed to know ahead of time. 'You will not know until the morning of the day.' Mmmmm, therefore Wednesday is the last possible day, but Wednesday is out out out the window because if you did not have it by Tuesday, you would know by Tuesday you would have it on Wednesday. And so. On and on and on until the end of time. See. It will never happen. So.

Joe What?

Bill So he will never come! Mr Rawlinson, if he phones on the morning of the day, he will never come! The paradox of the unexpected exam! You see! You see!

Bill is triumphant. Joe gets up and crosses over into his garden. He lunges at the carefully balanced rock and pushes it over. He turns to Bill –

Joe I hate you.

Bill starts humming. The hum builds to a crescendo. He turns on Joe and yells. Joe runs away

TWENTY-FOUR

*Front room: Joe, being interviewed by a Policeman.
Michelle, holding Joe's hand.*

Policeman You say he'd been to the skip?

Joe Yes.

Policeman And he didn't see anything unusual?

Joe No. Just chairs and that, he said.

Policeman What was his reaction when you told him
about Billy?

Joe Nothing much.

Policeman He didn't have any reaction?

Joe Not really, no. He just said –

Policeman Yes?

Joe He got confused. His name's Billy too.

Policeman And did he make any advance to you? At the
time?

Joe No, not then.

Policeman What happened next?

Joe He changed the subject.

Policeman To?

Joe The Fibonacci sequence.

Pause.

Policeman Is that a film?

Joe No. It's a maths thing. And then he talked about
wheels and circles and how they go round but some bits
go faster than others and all that stuff.

Policeman Why did he talk to you about these things?

Joe He thought I was interested, I suppose.

Policeman Were you?

Joe Yeah, well, they were interesting. And I thought he was interested in me. I mean, I didn't – I don't mean *that*. (*He starts getting upset.*) He just liked talking to me.

Michelle He's getting upset again, officer.

Policeman It's alright, you just take your time, son.

Joe I'm alright.

Policeman Did he make you feel uncomfortable, talking about these things?

Joe No. Not uncomfortable, no. It was like, he'd talk about equations and that, and it felt like the most important thing in the world, it was exciting, but then he started talking about Mum, and, I don't know why, but suddenly he was saying these terrible things about her, going on and on –

Policeman What kind of things?

Joe He was calling her names and stuff and no, I put my hands over my ears and then he started . . .

Policeman Go on.

Joe He put his hand here . . . on my chest. And I wasn't wearing a top – it was hot – and he put his hand here and . . . oh, Mum.

> *He collapses and turns to Michelle. She holds on to him for a moment, then releases him and steadies him.*

Michelle It's alright, Joe, it's alright.

Joe He put his hand here and then he stroked me down here all the way and then he put his hand, his other hand . . . and he said . . . he started . . . he said he wanted to . . . that he'd like to . . . he said he wanted me to go upstairs with him to his bedroom and . . . do it. (*He starts to cry.*)

Policeman Have a glass of squash, lad.

Joe drinks.

When you're ready.

Joe I'm ready.

Policeman What happened next?

Joe Mum came out.

Policeman And he told you about the incident?

Michelle Not at the time, no.

Policeman Did you tell anyone about the incident?

Joe No. I felt – I was . . .

Policeman You were . . . ?

Joe But the thing is –

Policeman Yes?

Joe The thing is –

Policeman Yes?

Joe I saw him, on the night Billy disappeared, I saw him.

Policeman Where?

Joe I didn't think anything of it at the time, but I saw him in the garden, in the middle of the night, I saw him *digging*.

Policeman Digging. In the middle of the night?

Joe Yes.

Policeman And what were you doing up? In the middle of the night?

Joe He woke me up.

Policeman Digging?

Joe Making noises. And digging, yeah, but making weird noises, he makes weird noises.

Policeman What kind of noises?

Joe Humming noises.

Policeman Like?

Joe Like hmmmn . . .

Policeman And he makes these noises often, does he?

Joe When he's vexed he does, yeah.

Policeman And would you say he was vexed while he was digging?

Joe Yeah.

Policeman Were you aware of this nocturnal activity, Mrs Rawlinson?

Michelle I wasn't aware of anything. I mean, he did say things, some of the things he said were well weird, but I didn't put two and two together, did I? I know I'm crap at maths, but you never think, you never like to think of your neighbour like that, do you? I just thought he was, you know, a bit soft.

Policeman Don't you punish yourself now. With hindsight we'd all be perfect witnesses.

Michelle What are you going to do?

Policeman Well . . .

Michelle He won't open the door. He never answers the door.

Policeman We'll be taking him in for questioning in due course.

Michelle You could go round the back if you like. Through the garden.

Policeman Don't you worry about that. We have means of forcing entrance in the event of non-compliance.

Michelle Only don't bring him round here, will you? You have to keep him away, keep him away from Joe.

Policeman We always do our utmost to ensure that witness and suspect are kept apart while the investigation is still under way.

Michelle You think he did it, then?

Policeman We don't know anything for certain yet, Mrs Rawlinson.

Michelle And all the time just *living* there like a normal person. I feel such a twat. We invited him round and everything.

Policeman I understand your apprehension and we are taking these accusations very seriously. But until we have interviewed Mr Tyler it is too early to make any retrospective judgements.

Joe I'm not lying.

Policeman No one's saying you are, Joe.

Joe I just didn't think – at the time – I just didn't think anything of it. But when he touched me and everything, I suddenly realised, I suddenly thought, it's him, it's *him*. And with the news and all that, going on at me about if anyone *knew* anything, if anyone *saw* anything, I thought,

I *knew* Billy and I *saw* Mr T and then he did that to me, and Billy was my friend and I didn't know what to do, I mean, if my dad was here he'd have gone round and sorted him out, but then I thought I should tell you, that that was the right thing to do. That's why.

Policeman You did the right thing, Joe.

Michelle starts to cry. The Policeman offers her a tissue.

Michelle Thank you, officer.

Policeman I'll leave you two alone for a bit. Do you mind if I use the facilities?

Michelle Go ahead. First on the right.

Michelle continues to cry.

Joe Why are you crying, Mum?

Michelle Oh, Joe.

Joe He didn't give *me* a tissue.

Michelle You want one?

She passes him one. They both sit in silence, vacant.

TWENTY-FIVE

Street corner. Clint.

Clint Probability is not a science. Chances are, depends on who you are. Forget *statistics*, I'm talking about *character*. Chances are, Jip would say, all men are out to do you. That's what Jip would say. That's his experience. And given his experience, he's got a point. But it's *his* point, right, it's not my point or your point, it's his point and he's on the sharp end of it, so fair point. Yes. But not

85

mine. And *their* point is: where was Bill at ten a.m. on August 3rd? Chances are, they always say, chances are it's someone they know. We've all heard the statistics. Chances are, it's someone in their family, an acquaintance, a neighbour, a friend, it's not the lollipop man with a large net in a white van, is it? Bill lives in the same street, and no one knows what he was doing at the time of the crime. No one ever knows what he's doing any time, because he doesn't know anybody. Except me. That's the point. And statistically speaking, in all probability, as Bill himself would say, it's him then, isn't it? But I'm saying he was with me. Which is a lie. I hadn't met him then because this was the week before I met him. But I'm not telling them the truth. Because the truth in this case is wrong. The truth is, he was talking to the boy next door who was doing karate but the boy next door doesn't appear to remember. And Bill knows that I'm saying he was with me, but he insists he was in his garden which proves he couldn't have done it because he can't lie to save his life. But this isn't a question of him being guilty. Anyone can see he wouldn't hurt a daisy. This is a question of *things that stick*. And meanwhile, as a consequence of their lack of evidence, the clever men in blue have put their clever heads together and come up with the clever conclusion that, if I'm a liar, the chances are I might also be a murderer. Well, you can understand it. From their point of view, they've got their targets. But they're in the wrong total fucking arena. They'll never find him, whoever did it, with that logic. They should be interviewing men with office jobs. They want to be asking questions of civil servants, salesmen, captains of industry living in fake Tudor houses with the same haircuts they had when they were nine. The kind of person they're looking for, he'll be married, going to work every day, bored out of his head, nice house, fat car, big garden, wife like a fridge. You look at your history of psychopaths, they're all bored. Bored people are dangerous. We, on the other hand, are far too cold, hungry, thirsty, or off our ugly faces to be bored. You're living *in extremis*, you don't have the energy to go round killing people. But I've got my alibis. I'm alright. Don't worry about me. I can take the stick. But Bill? Eggs on the doorstep. Broken windows. He doesn't understand it, why should he? And Saturday morning, regular as clockwork, he is, this Saturday, where is he? That's my concern. He didn't turn up. Where else would he go? He's on his own, Bill. And that's no place to be when the rabble can't find anyone to fit their noose.

TWENTY-SIX

Train. Liza and Henry. Liza returns to her seat.

Henry What did he say? Was he pleased?

Liza He's dead.

Henry No.

Liza Yes, Henry, he's dead.

Henry Did you push him?

Liza Of course I didn't push him. He jumped.

Henry Why?

Liza That 'passenger action on the line'. It was him.

Henry Why would he do that?

Liza I didn't get to say sorry.

Henry That's not why he jumped.

Liza Do you think he heard us?

Henry No.

Liza We'll never know now.

Henry What?

Liza Whether he did it.

Henry Well, he didn't steal my pen.

Liza If it wasn't him, *who was it*?

Henry It's the wrong question. The question is why? Why would anyone want to murder an innocent?

Liza But if it wasn't him, why did he jump?

Henry Because he was weird, unhappy, ugly, I don't know. Forget about him.

Liza It doesn't make sense.

Henry Logic can only take you from A to B. Imagination / can take you anywhere.

Liza I don't want to go anywhere. I want to go home.

Henry Oh no.

Liza What?

Henry Those windmills.

Liza Well, they're better than nuclear power stations. That's what they say.

Henry No. It's those windmills again.

Liza Don't be silly. All windmills look the same.

Henry And that house with the green door. The bridge!

Liza Oh yes. I recognise that.

Henry I can't bear it. We're going back the way we came.

Liza Home! Hooray. (*She stands up*). Stand up.

Henry I'm not happy any more. I don't want to stand up.

Liza Happiness is not the only reason for standing up. Come on.

He stands up. Liza ushers him round into her seat.

There.

Henry What did you do that for?

Liza Now you're going forwards.

Henry But you're going backwards.

Liza I don't mind. Someone's always got to go backwards for someone else to go forwards. I don't mind.

TWENTY-SEVEN

Back yard. Joe, practising karate. Bill walks into the garden. He plants a FOR SALE *sign in the ground. He ignores Joe. Joe stops suddenly on seeing Bill. He's afraid to move. Bill stops and stares at him. They continue to stare at each other in silence for a while. Suddenly Bill crosses to Joe. He goes right up to him, studying his face intently. Silence.*

Bill Why?

Joe is unable to speak. Eventually, Bill turns and walks away. Joe remains.
Next door, Bill puts on his hat and coat. He fetches a suitcase.

TWENTY-EIGHT

Train. Henry and Liza.
 Henry reaches for a banana and starts peeling it.

Liza What are you doing?

Henry I'm eating a banana.

Liza You've never eaten a banana before in your life.

Henry I have examined my aversion and found it to be nothing more than prejudice.

 Silence. He continues to eat.

Liza Do you like it?

Henry No.

 He continues eating.

TWENTY-NINE

Michelle appears in the doorway of their house. She calls to Joe.

Michelle Joe! Your dad called. Usual bollocks about work and not having enough money and time and all that crap, but he's nearly finished his job, then he'll be able to see you, he says.

 Joe doesn't move.

Oy. I said your dad wants to see you.

 Pause.

Joe Why?

Michelle What?

Joe Now?

Michelle Don't be stupid. When he's finished this job, he says.

Joe When's that?

Michelle No idea. You know what he's like. He'll call again when he's finished. First day he gets off, he said.

Joe But when will that be?

Michelle I don't know, do I? On the day.

Joe *What day?*

Michelle Don't get mardy with me. I'm just telling you. He won't know until he's finished. He'll call the day, on the day he's gonna come, alright?

She goes back inside. Silence. Joe looks into the horizon, willing his dad to appear.
Bill picks up his suitcase and walks into the distance.

The End.